What Others Are Saying

"*Living Your Extreme Destiny* is such a heartening read. No matter where you are in life, there is something for you to grab hold of and use to improve your life. Through sharing her life and her journey with God, Toni reveals truths and rock-solid advice that applies to everyone, especially young women. Pick up your copy, and you will be inspired, challenged and validated. It's a valuable addition to any bookshelf. I highly recommend it to everyone."

—Katryna Johnson, JD, Founder and CEO of
Mirelli Entrepreneur Training for Women

"Authentically bold yet spiritually awakening, *Living Your Extreme Destiny* exposes the vulnerabilities and bridging of personal growth. Toni C. Hughes provides both a blueprint and testimony of her journey to inspire others to reign their destiny with God at the helm. Each chapter imparts strategies for elevating within your chosen craft, providing fresh perspectives of positive life change. I highly recommend this as an essential read for everyone as they navigate through life's course."

—Nikki-Qui Brown, EdD, Director of Law
Enforcement Training Academy

"*Living Your Extreme Destiny* is an eye opener. The author, Toni C. Hughes, shines a very bright light on the importance of knowing who you are and understanding your purpose in life. She very bravely displayed the troubles and negatives of her own life, which enables one to see that although your journey may start bumpy or uncertain, it can and will always lead to success when following God. Each mountain, hill, or valley will lead you safely on. You must remember to place God in charge. I highly recommend that everyone wondering "who and what I am" to read this book and see it as a blueprint for their lives.

—Rev. Eunice D. Freeman, EdD, LMSW

Living Your Extreme DESTINY

A Guide to Defining, Understanding, and Living Your Passion

TONI C. HUGHES

WESTBOW
PRESS®
A DIVISION OF THOMAS NELSON
& ZONDERVAN

WestBow Press books may be ordered through booksellers or by contacting:

WestBow Press
A Division of Thomas Nelson & Zondervan
1663 Liberty Drive
Bloomington, IN 47403
www.westbowpress.com
844-714-3454

All Scripture quotations are taken from The Holy Bible, New
International Version®, NIV® Copyright © 1973, 1978, 1984, 2011 by
Biblica, Inc.® Used by permission. All rights reserved worldwide.

Cover photo credit: Michelle Bryant Griffin

ISBN: 978-1-6642-1138-4 (sc)
ISBN: 978-1-6642-1139-1 (hc)
ISBN: 978-1-6642-1140-7 (e)

Library of Congress Control Number: 2020921656

Print information available on the last page.

WestBow Press rev. date: 12/17/2020

Is This Book for You?

If you are open-minded and in need of guidance on how to find your true worth and value, this book is for you. If you are in a rut or stuck in a place of fear, not knowing what you were placed on this earth to do, this book is for you. If you have found your passion but don't know your purpose, then this book is for you. If you are confused or lost in the world and don't know why you were created, this book is for you. If you are working a dead-end job and want to know your calling, this book is for you. You are in good company. If you are someone who knows what your passion is and want to bless someone else with direction and guidance on how to discover and live their passion and just don't know how to say it or approach them, this book is for you and them. Be someone who not only gets fed by the words of this book but share this book with others. If you find you have all the answers to living your passion and having a completely fulfilled life, use this book for reference. If this book is for you, I encourage you to read it and tell someone else about it, to help them find their true calling and purpose on this earth. By doing this, you will be helping someone grow as an individual, which will ultimately help improve your life as well.

To those who are in search of why they were created.

For the person who has doubts and uncertainties about themselves and their gifts.

You have the tools inside of you to reach your extreme destiny and have the life you deserve.

You can do this. I believe in you!

To my daughter, Malayia, and my son, Malik. Live your passion to the full. I value you.

Most importantly, to that young person who desires to become all that God has created them to be. You are loved.

CONTENTS

FOREWORD

It takes a whole lot of courage to look deep into your life and discover what has worked and what hasn't worked. It takes even more courage, or shall I say a whole lot of moxie, to then turn around and share your life's story with others.

This is exactly what Toni Hughes has done in her book, *Living Your Extreme Destiny*. In this writing, Toni holds nothing back. She shares her journey to discovering her unique, authentic self and how she was able to pull together the broken pieces of her life and allow God to heal her heart. Because only then can you truly experience the radical transformation that Toni shares about her life.

Written with a lot of honesty, courage, and inspiration, Toni, step-by-step, shows the readers how they, too, can move beyond their old stories and rewrite a new story that reflects who they really are.

The truth is we all have had our share of pain, disappointments, and betrayals. It's a part of all of our stories. But what makes our stories unique is how we find the strength, the courage, and the fight to keep going and never give up. This is what Toni has done and clearly demonstrates in this book.

Toni reveals how we all have the power to change our lives as she reveals her own struggles and the processes she used to find her truth and her passion. And speaking of passion, Toni has found hers. Now she's on a mission to help others do the same.

This is exactly what she's done in *Living Your Extreme Destiny*. I encourage you to delve deeply into the pages of this powerful book and use it as a guide to propel you into your true passion and destiny.

We all are born with a divine plan and purpose for our lives. When we discover this plan and purpose, our lives take on new meaning of infinite possibility. Toni has stepped into her divine plan, and now she's living out her purpose and passion through her gifts, talents, and amazing body of work.

As you read each page, understand that not only is it possible to live your extreme destiny, it's inevitable with the right kind of support.

Toni has become your support through the pages of this phenomenal book.

I salute you, Toni, for your courage, your strength, and your inspiration to help others live their dreams and passion.

—Angela Carr Patterson, Global Life and Success Strategist

PREFACE

It was what seemed like a long day at McKissack Middle School. I was about eleven or twelve years old. Thankfully, I made it to school, even though just that morning I had thrown up, and feeling my forehead told me that I was burning up. I was only alert enough to get out of bed and force myself to get dressed that morning so that I wouldn't miss anything that the school could teach me and keep my perfect attendance record. I wanted to learn it all, even in the midst of feeling ill and down. I had never missed a day of middle school and loved to learn as much as possible. I was eager to get to school that day, just as I was any other day of the school week. My mom had no clue what I was up to, as she was still asleep. As I made it to school and sat in my chair, I could barely answer the teacher as I heard my name being called to roll call to see who was in attendance. My teacher promptly got out of her chair and approached me, as she didn't hear me answer, "Here," when she called my name. I was out of it. But that feeling of knowing that I was present had me so determined that I was going to stay at school that day. To my surprise, the teacher walked me to the principal's office only to call my mom and send me home. I was devastated and cried all the way home, resisting my mom as she pulled me out of school that day.

Till this day, I remember that day at school, and I remember going to the school board of education with my complaint when I didn't receive my award for perfect attendance because of missing that day of school. That is just how determined I was to learn and to receive the honor of perfect attendance. I was a little determined young lady and wanted to be great. Would you like to know why I was so determined? Let me explain.

When I was a young child, I experienced growing up in the projects, better known as government-funded housing, on the welfare system in Nashville, Tennessee. My parents never married and didn't live together. I had four brothers and one sister. Two of my older brothers lived with my dad. I lived with my mother, younger sister, younger brother, and an older brother. My mother suffered from a drug addiction, and as a result, my brothers, my sister, and I were neglected. I can remember being in elementary school and missing a lot of days because my mom wasn't in her right mind to make sure we got to school. It was in the first grade when I got left behind due to too many missed days.

As I got older, I took on the primary role of mother, sister, and guardian of my younger brother and sister for some time while living with our mom. I can remember not being able to get in the house and having to climb in a window just to get inside. I watched my mom being physically abused and taken advantage of by men. I also remember seeing needles lying around in her bedroom the times I snuck in to see what I could learn about her. There were times we didn't have food, and I went to school feeling ashamed of our living situation. Also, there were times in school when I would just keep to myself to avoid talking about what went on in my home. I even heard helicopters and gunfire some nights while I was up trying to do homework. One day, I saw a man get shot in broad daylight. It was terrifying, and I knew that I didn't want to live like that. I used to dance with my cousin as my little brother would make jokes, just to keep our minds off the pain and things that went on at home. That feeling, that environment, and that living situation made me determined to live a different life than what my mom lived. I wanted something better.

When my mother could no longer care for us, we moved in with my dad, which is when my relationship with God became a part of who I am to this day. My dad was a minister and a truck driver. He drove his truck for twenty-two years, accident-free. This accomplishment made me proud. This was the beginning of a new start for me, and I was excited. Can you imagine?

While in high school, I made a decision that I would do the opposite of the negative things I saw my mom do and lead a life that represents what God wants for me. I wanted to reach the highest degree of success as possible. I wanted to live my extreme destiny. Here is where my motivation began.

ACKNOWLEDGMENTS

I would first like to acknowledge God and thank him for everything inspired by his Word that helped me write this book. I would like to thank my mom, Betty, for teaching me about respect. I have learned that you should speak before entering someone's home. This is one of the traits about me that I admire and love. This is an important trait to have and receive if you want to live your best life. I would like to thank my bonus mom, Gail, for helping me go beyond the norm and move so that I could grow as an individual. If we stay within a box, we will not be able to develop into the person God created us to be. I would like to thank my grandmother for inspiring me to be happy. She taught me what strength is and how to endure as a woman. I would like to thank my father for instilling wisdom and God in my life. I don't know what I would have done without my father. Thanks, Dad, for treating me like I am the prettiest girl in the world and for teaching me that I can be anything I want to be. I would like to thank my best friend, Vanessa, for inspiring and encouraging me. Your words mean so much, and you are dynamic. I am grateful to call you friend. I would like to thank George McCarter. You helped me identify the areas of my life that I needed help with. You gave me resources and guidance in my journey throughout my senior year of high school. Your support helped shape me into the person I am. I would like to thank Barry Scott. You taught me that I had what it takes to be an actor. You made me believe in myself because you believed in me. Without you guys, there would be no me, and for that I am grateful to you all.

For those who supported me in the development of this book, I am eternally grateful to the following:

- Langley Watts Cornell, for encouraging me to open up and talk about the hard topics that once had me in bondage
- The Rough Writers, for helping with your constructive critique for the writings of this book
- WestBow Press for believing in me

To my readers, thank you!

INTRODUCTION
ARE YOU READY?

Greatness exists in all of us.
—Will Smith

Have you ever wondered what the meaning of your life was? Have you ever reached a certain milestone only to realize that you haven't figured out who you are or why you were placed on this earth? Or have you thought that maybe it's too late? Have you given up on life? Have you ever thought about what you do that gives you extreme happiness? Do you know what your gift is? Could you imagine what it would be like to have all the answers to the questions about your purpose in your life? Have you had any thoughts about who you are and what God had in mind when you were created?

All of these questions are things that you or someone you know has thought about. These are definitely questions that I once had and wanted answered. I wanted to know the meaning of my life and why I was created. There is a reason for everything, and you better believe I was curious to know. I wanted answers. I wanted to know who I was. I wanted to know my purpose and meaning in life. This would be the answer to my life's purpose, and I could breathe and relax once my questions were answered.

Don't you want to know why you were born? So what are you waiting for? Buckle up and enjoy the ride. Let's get started with this journey of discovery!

My Motivation

The world we live in today is consumed with crime, bitterness, anger, resentment, and suicide. *Living Your Extreme Destiny* was written as I was in pursuit of my purpose in life. I had just had a birthday and was living an unfulfilled life. I was desperate to know what my reason for being put here on earth was, and I'm sure some of you have had the same thought or know someone who has. I knew that God had something better for my life, and I wanted to know what that was. I believe if people live within their purpose, the hate, crime, and suicide rates will decrease. Have you ever wondered what it would be like to live at a capacity where you had complete happiness and self-worth? Where you were valued at the highest? Where your life had meaning? Where you had a reason for living? When you can identify your purpose and meaning in life, you have an advantage that most don't have. *You become extreme in existence. You become.*

The world we live in is full of hate, unhappiness, chaos, and pain. Just imagine if there was peace, love, and happiness—and people had fulfilled lives that they enjoyed. When you have the tools and resources to grab hold of what and who you are, you can soar.

This guide will open up ways to find out what and who you are destined to be and what you can become on an extreme level.

As you navigate the pages of this book, keep an open mind and view on why you exist. With wisdom, knowledge, and understanding, you will get out of this book what you are open and willing to receive. God will not give you what you ask for, only what you can manage and what you deserve. Think about it. When you pray, does God always give you what you ask for? No, he doesn't because he knows what we can handle and what we are ready for. He has all the answers and is our creator, so he knows what's best for us. In this book, you will learn tips on how to find your gift and passion and how to find your purpose in life. You will learn how to use your gifts and talents to influence the world. With every ounce in me, I pray that God grants you your heart's desire and opens up doors for you to live your extreme destiny. You are my motivation!

CHAPTER 1

Uncovering Your Unique You

Challenges make you discover things about
yourself that you never really knew.
—Cicely Tyson

I t was a warm and sunny day at Pearl Cohn High. It was
my sophomore year, and we were well into the school year.
I wasn't the typical sixteen-year-old girl, as I was dressed
in my normal baggy blue jeans, a T-shirt, and what we called
tennis shoes or sneakers. I was definitely a tomboy growing up
with four brothers and only one sister. With my hair slicked
back in my regular ponytail, I hung out with the guys all the
time and stayed to myself for most of the school day. This was a
daily routine for me, and it was how I liked it. It was what I was
comfortable with—until I saw something that made me jump
for joy. I saw a group of girls dancing, and it reminded me of
my younger days when I was happy. I saw the majorette squad,
better known as the dance team, that danced during halftime
of football games. I built up the courage to try out for the
team, and the next thing I knew, I was approached by one of
the dancers, who told me that they wanted me. I was delighted!
After I made the team and had several performances, I also
tried out for the squad that performed during halftime of
basketball games, and I made that team as well! That was the
beginning of uncovering who I really was underneath all the

shame, hurt, and pain. This new reveal made me realize that I was born to entertain in some shape or form.

There were some essential things that took place during that time for me. First, I was comfortable being a tomboy until I rediscovered my early childhood love of dancing and entertaining. I had to change my attitude about dressing with baggy clothes and dress like a young lady in a leotard! Ouch! That was a strange feeling initially, but I eventually got used to it. I also had to wear some makeup and tights, which took some getting used to. I had to wear my hair down, so no more ponytails. Oh my! All of this made me realize that I had to change my mind-set regarding the way I looked and dressed. I wanted to do what it took to be the best dancer, so determination took over.

This applies to anything new that you may be experiencing. Maybe you have thought about joining a new social club or becoming a part of a special team or doing something that reminds you of your younger years. In order to learn who you really are underneath all the things you have experienced, you have to dig deep within and uncover the real you, uncover the true you, your unique you. So uncover. You can do this!

Another thing I learned during my uncovering was the fact that I was a natural leader. I was always asked to be in a position of leadership. I was the captain of the volleyball and track teams, and I really enjoyed encouraging my teammates to help us stay motivated. It was a team effort, and our coach was all for it. I couldn't figure out why I was always asked to be the captain, but I decided that I had the attitude of a leader.

In order to uncover your unique you, you will need three things: attitude, mind-set, and determination. You want to aim for a positive attitude and mind-set. You also have to have a certain drive and willpower that brings in the determination aspect. Let's look at what each word means:

Attitude—a settled way of thinking or feeling about someone or something, typically reflected in a person's behavior.

Mind-set—the established set of attitudes held by someone.

Determination—firmness of purpose, resoluteness.

You have to have an attitude that allows you to be open to learning or relearning what's already in you from childhood or what you have been taught. If you have a negative attitude, you will get a negative result. Your outcome is a reflection of your attitude. Have a positive attitude. If you say you're going to have a bad day, you will have a bad day. If you say you're going to have a good day, you will have a good day. Your *mind-set* is a reflection of your attitude. If your mind-set is stuck on limiting beliefs, you will decline and hinder your growth. You want to work on removing limiting beliefs and replacing them with limitless beliefs.

You may also need to change your mind-set about this adventure so that you are welcoming to it. If you want to excel, you must have *determination* to stand out from the crowd. When something is embedded or deeply rooted within you, you have to be determined to pull it out so that you can soar! Don't resist that feeling you once had as a small child. Let your imagination flow so that you can be you in your own unique way. For instance, when I was in high school and realized my capabilities, I wanted to be involved in as many activities as possible. I tried out for almost every activity you can do in high school. I was a student first and made sure to keep my grades up so that my dad would approve of me being in extracurricular activities. I was extremely determined.

So who are you really? What makes you stand out? How do you peel off the layers to find who you are underneath? To find the inner being that tells you why you were created, you must first discover your gift.

Discovering Your Gifts

What makes you special? What makes you stand out? What is that one thing you have that no one can take away? What is your calling? What is your gift? What problem can you solve with your gift? What makes you different? What makes you a leader? What were you born to do?

Being special sets you apart from others. Not in a bad or unaccepting way but in a way that allows you to be an inspiration or have an impact on others. It really depends on how you use what you have. The good news is that you are divine in your own way, so take that to heart and take advantage of that. It's what makes you stand out and what gives people insight into the real you. What makes you stand out is the one thing that gives you your uniqueness. Be original in all you do, and only use others as a guide to push you to your next level. Don't be afraid to tap into that. Your gift is the one thing that no one can take away from you—always remember that.

It is what allows you to be an inspiration and make a difference in the world. Your calling is the thing that God created you to do. It could be helping women who have a dysfunctional relationship with their mom overcome that and succeed in life. Having a gift can open the door for you to have the opportunity to solve a problem. You could be a major difference maker in the world. Your uniqueness is what makes you different. If we were all the same, it would be a boring place. What makes you a leader is the fact that you can tap into your gift and use it to help others in some way. Then people will begin to look up to you. You were born to be a leader in your gift, so don't stop at anything to find out what that is.

When I was around three or four, I was in church because of my dad and grandmother. This was during the time my mom and dad were still together, before my mom started using drugs. I remember watching my dad and other church members rebuking an evil spirit that was in a lady at the church. Her eyes were big, and she seemed to be in some type of element or space. I watched her as they rebuked and renounced this evil spirit out of her. It was a unique thing to see, and the average person wouldn't believe it unless they saw it themselves. That day made me a believer.

As I got older and attended church like my life depended on it, I learned that I could sing. When I learned this, I was only singing church songs in our church choir. I eventually became the lead in our church choir. Then, ultimately, I became the choir director. This was something that I enjoyed doing. It was the gateway to healing for my soul as I overcame every obstacle placed in front of me on my journey. I learned that God blessed me with more than one gift. Throughout my whole childhood, I sang in church. I loved it, and it was something that kept me close to God. In my youth, I also discovered that I could draw. I never really put a title to what type of artist I was, but I had the ability to look at another drawing and draw from that, mostly cartoon characters and basic objects. I thought that was cool. These are a few gifts that I was born with. I had no formal training or guidance. These things came naturally to me, and I gravitated to them easily.

Your gift is what you were born with. It is your source of significance. No one can take away what God naturally blessed you with. That makes you special. How do you discover your gift? Think back to your childhood. What were some of the things that interested you? What were you naturally good at? Have you ever lost track of time? If so, what were you doing? If you can answer these questions, you can get an idea of what your gift is.

Your gift is your key to everything. Once you have discovered your gift, don't focus on becoming successful. Instead, *focus on becoming a person of value*. If you take this approach, success will come. You will go far. You will add meaning to your life and know that you are enough. You must discover your gift in order to be fulfilled. Your gift helps shape you into the person God created you to be. When you discover your gift, you can make it anywhere. Your gift is embedded within you. It is your pathway to freedom. Your gift is your strength, and it protects you from a lot of negativity. Keep in mind that people don't have to like you, but they may just like what you have to offer in your gift. They could also just like your potential of what you can be. I can remember times when people would be so excited to see photos of me using my gift, but when they would see me in person, they would ignore me or not respond to my phone calls or text messages. But they would be overjoyed to hear about the new film I was in or the new opportunity I had to use my gift. I had to brush that off and keep pushing. My mentor said to me once, "Adverse situations reveal true character," but you must keep your eye on what you were created to do. Use your gift to the full, regardless of the obstacles. Don't be afraid to shine. The world needs to see what you have to offer. You have something special, and I know that you can do anything and become all that you were created to be. Now it's time for you to accept who you are and stop waiting and procrastinating. It is your season to shine. So tap into your gift like your life depends on it, and you will have the initial experience of what it is like to maximize your life to the full. I believe in you! You can and will exceed your day-to-day normal expectations when you are living in your dreams and operating in your gift. This is the beginning of living your extreme destiny.

Discovering your gift will make you unstoppable. When I discovered that I could entertain an audience, I didn't stop there. I continued to entertain throughout high school, college, and beyond. You can do the same. It is the essence of who you really are and why you were born. You can take this gift and use it to your benefit. Let it be your reason for living—your reason for being a person of value. Your gift is your ticket to freedom. It makes you stand out in the crowd, granting you your right to be all you can be. It is to your benefit, so take advantage of it and max it out. When I discovered my gift, I became free from other people controlling me. I became me. Simply. Me. For instance, when I became pregnant with my first child, my dad told me I had to get married, and he made it very clear that I could not bring a child in this world without being married. I remembered all the things I had learned from him and from being in church, and I obeyed my father and got married while pregnant at age twenty-one. Well, later, that marriage failed. Even though my dad had good intentions and wanted what was best for me, I allowed him to control my situation even though I was an adult. At that time, I didn't know my purpose or the value of my gifts. I didn't know what I know now, so I didn't discover my true calling until the writing of this book several years later. Now that I have the power of my gift and I am operating in my purpose, no one can control me but God. We have to live for us and stay in alignment with what God has for our life. Our parents want the best for us, but we have control over our destiny, and only God has the kind of power to make us move when he says move. God is my strength through every obstacle, challenge, doubt, and anything that may be a block. You can overcome anything if you put your faith in you and know that you are powerful! Uncover your gift so that you can soar!

Uncover that part of you that has been closed up in a box and limited to only what view you thought you had. Open your eyes to limitless possibilities when you maximize your faith in yourself and in your capabilities. You are gifted. Now take that gift and run with it so fast. You are important. You are special. You are valuable. I know you are capable of unlocking the gem that lives within to get the life you desire and deserve. You're only limited to what you think, so don't let anything or anyone stop you from reaching the level of life you're supposed to have by utilizing your gift. Run with it and explode!

I suspect you're wondering why I am so passionate about your gift. I believe that your gift is the one thing that you have that can open up the pathway to living your extreme destiny. It is the one thing that gives you the advantage that will allow you to be you! It is the one thing that will open up several opportunities that will help increase your value. It makes you a leader! Everyone is born with a gift, and if you shine in it, you can lead others.

Just imagine. You have discovered your gift and are living it out, and others see you and see how happy and fulfilled you are. You then can show leadership in the gift that you have because that is what makes you unique. Yes. Think about it. If you operate in your gift, you dominate that area, and that makes you the leader. Therefore, you are born a leader. Everyone is. Once you tap into your purpose for living, you will be admired, and people will want to come to you, and you can serve in the area of your gifting. You will then be living your extreme destiny!

You want to make sure you are not just living. You don't want to die and have lived a life that doesn't reflect what you were made to do. Maximize your gift to the unthinkable degree that no one can explain. Give yourself the key to open the door that leads to your destiny. You deserve to live the best life that you possibly can. Open your eyes to who you really are. Open your heart to who you can become. Open your mind and believe that you are destined for greatness.

Knowing Your Talents

As Melony sat on the sofa sipping her tea, she realized that it was the beginning of the day and she was just getting ready to start her day. She thought about all the hard work she had put in her collection of women's clothes for her upcoming new clothing line. She was excited and eager to have her collection displayed in the upcoming fashion show in Paris. As she began to sketch out some new designs, she realized that she had reached the level of success that proved she was talented in her craft, and she wanted desperately to grow into all that God wanted her to be. With that said, she began to get to work with scheduling times to meet her models for a run through. This was the life she had always dreamed of.

Gifts can become talents. Your talent is God's gift to you. A talent is something that someone has, a natural ability to be good at something. So my ability to sing is not only a gift, it's also a talent. I remember watching talent shows as a way to learn what a talent really was. Some people would sing, dance, quote poetry, or do stand-up comedy. It was an interesting experience, and I learned a lot from watching it. One thing I would like to add is that it is an extreme pleasure to use my talent to honor God. So those times I sang in the choir were very comforting experiences. It brought a love that could only be understood if you understand the Holy Spirit. That's how talent works. It's not like a skill, which is something that is learned. It is something that comes naturally to you. What is your talent? What is something that you are naturally gifted with? You can use your gift and talent to fulfill a purpose. But first, the goal is to fulfill God's purpose for your life and glorify him. Maybe you are a fashion designer like Melony. Maybe you are a dancer or singer. Whatever talent you have, just remember that you are special, and you deserve to express your abilities to fulfill your destiny.

Being of Service

Congratulations! You have discovered your gifts and talents. That is one of the most important steps in finding your way to reaching your extreme destiny. Now it's time to put them into action and tap into what's next—being of service. Yes, you need to know your gifts and talents for your life, but you also need to think about how you can be of service to others by using your gifts and talents. One way is being active in your local church. You could also be a member of an organization that serves the community. It's important to serve because it allows you to be selfless. Not thinking about yourself or making it seem like it's all about you will set you apart from those who only think of themselves or are always trying to get something out of the deal. There is nothing wrong with taking care of your needs and taking care of yourself, but don't forget about the less fortunate and those who are in need. You can make a huge difference in someone's life if you can think of them when they need it the most. For instance, I created assignments for Sunday school lessons in our family church. I was the church treasurer and secretary at one point. I was of service to my church, which honors God. Maybe you could be a part of a nonprofit and use your gifts and talents to uplift others who are in need during a troubling time in their lives. You just never know what you could do to inspire someone else.

Your gift is not for you; it's to be used as a service to others. Find favor in your serving as you use the gift that you were born with. You are important, and so are those in need.

Being Yourself

There was a girl who was always looking out the window of the airplane. She always wanted to know what it would be like to live the life of a celebrity. There was this particular celebrity she admired. The celebrity was an upbeat, positive, outgoing girl who grew up in the suburbs and now lived in a mansion in Los Angeles, California. She wore designer clothes and always had the latest hairstyles and nail art. She was fabulous. The girl who was always looking out the window of the airplane, however, was an introvert and spent her time reading books, going to the library, and staying home for the most part. She led a very simple life and stayed to herself. She admired the celebrity and followed her every move on social media. She found herself going out more and dressing in name-brand clothing to be just like the celebrity. One day, the girl who always looked out the window learned that the celebrity had married another famous celebrity. This made the girl who always looked out the window excited! She thought she would do the same thing and marry the first guy who asked, only to find out that the guy was already married with three kids a month later. The girl who always looked out the window was devastated and regretted every decision she had made to follow in the footsteps of the celebrity.

Does that story sound familiar? Sometimes we can want to be like someone else so badly that we set ourselves up for failure. That's why it's important to know who you are and why you were created, so you can avoid the mistakes that the girl who was always looking out the window made and focus on finding your gifts and talents.

Now that you have found your gift and talents and have served others, let's talk about why it's important to be yourself. Sometimes when someone is talented, others tend to want to be like them so much that they neglect their own identity or forget who they are. They try so hard to keep up with the latest news on a certain individual or want to make sure they are aware of their every move.

There is no hiding. Be the same person in public that you are in private. Don't try to act a certain way for a certain expectation. Live with no expectations and don't be afraid to shine and show who you really are. Celebrate your accomplishments and then keep it moving to create more. Create and leave your legacy.

Don't try to imitate someone else. Be yourself. It's okay to learn from others, and more importantly, it's okay to watch and observe, but learn from others mistakes. I'm sure you can relate to the girl who was always looking out the window, but you can also learn a lesson from her as well.

You want to maintain your unique you so that you stand out in the crowd rather than fit in. Remember, everyone has a gift. Use that gift to be yourself. Don't fake it until you make it; be authentic so that you can become the best version of yourself. Being yourself will help you maintain your image. Staying focused on what is true to you and not doubting yourself will take you far. Dedicate some time to get to know yourself. You can plan a weekend alone, away from all the noise, and use that time to uncover who you really are and focus on your mind-set. Come on, you can do this!

Mind-Set

Your mind-set will determine the outcome of your success. It is one of the most—if not the most—important factors in reaching your extreme destiny. You want to have a champion's mind-set. Everything you do should be centered around your gift. Study your craft. When you know you have rehearsal, show up. Never disappoint yourself or others in the commitments you make. Have a mind-set of a go-getter. Be a team player. Face your demons and eliminate them. And, as an actor, when it's time for you to prepare for a role, you've got to put yourself in the mind-set of the character. You've got to remove yourself from the equation and go all in. It's all or nothing. Don't worry about how people see you. Focus. On. The. Task. At. Hand. Having a level of curiosity can help you grow as well. Don't stop. Don't let anything or anyone take your joy. Have the mind-set of moving forward in your efforts to achieve greatness while using your gift. Don't stop believing. Don't stop believing in yourself no matter what anyone says or does. You hold the key to living your extreme destiny. Ignore the opinions of others and focus on the things that are important. Make time for things that matter. Set your mind up to believe that you can stand out in a crowd. If that means taking classes or getting some extra training, do that. Put your mind-set in a space of determination and live with no expectations.

Live with No Expectations

Live with no expectations. If you can spend time on yourself, getting to know yourself, you should also consider not expecting anything from others. If you can keep focused on your task, whatever that is, you can rely on yourself and God. Don't rely on people. When you live with no expectations, you protect yourself in a way that you're responsible for your needs being met, and not others. You identify with yourself to a degree that you make you happy. Don't rely on anyone else for happiness. It is your responsibility to do the necessary things to make you okay and to make sure you are at your best as much as possible. What others bring to the table just adds to what you already have. Don't doubt yourself and understand that everyone makes mistakes; just make sure you are learning from your mistakes and not repeating them. You can do it. When you live with no expectations, you can't be let down. It allows for you to take sole responsibility for your outcome. So, if someone asks to borrow a hundred dollars from you and you know that this person has a history of not paying you back, then don't loan them the money, unless you know that you don't need it back. When you use this approach, you won't have any expectation of getting it back. But if they just so happen to give it back, then that's a plus! Living with no expectations eliminates the possibility of you getting angry or upset with someone. You have total control of the situation and the outcome, so that gives you the advantage. So keep in mind that when you live with no expectations, you have control of your destiny.

Having Limitless Faith

Have you ever prayed to God, only to get no response? Have you ever had doubt or disbelief about a certain matter? This is a common thing that happens to a lot of us, so if this fits you, don't feel like you're the only one. Begin to read your Bible with continuous prayer and meditation on his Word. Begin to ask God to give you faith that will allow you to have no limitations to the highest degree. You have to soar in your element if you want to live an extreme life. In order to soar, you want to have limitless faith. Hebrews 11:1 states, "Now faith is confidence in what we hope for and assurance about what we do not see" (NIV). Trust in God and know that he is with you. Put all your faith in him and give him your heart because he will not disappoint you. When the enemy attacks you, just know that God is the king and ruler over all and has the authority to defeat the enemy at any given moment. You are his seed, and you were made in his likeness, so you also have the authority to defeat the enemy. Use that to your advantage. Believe in him and believe in yourself. Have faith in yourself and know that you are the ruler of your craft. No one can take this away from you, so don't ever doubt that. Keeping God as the head of your life will put you in the arena to be undefeated when it comes to facing challenges. You just have to have faith in yourself, and I know you can do it. Don't stop believing in God, because he will not stop believing in you. He is a man of his word, so trust him and trust that he will help guide you to your destination of living your extreme destiny. If you can continue to have faith on a consistent basis, you will have limitless possibilities and overcome any situation.

Overcoming Hardship

If you have experienced any type of hardship, give yourself the opportunity to overcome the trauma, disappointments, and dysfunction you may have experienced in your life by first accepting it. Avoid the blame game. No one is perfect, and everything happens for a reason, so allow yourself to look in the mirror and think about how you feel about what happened and how you're going to handle it. Work on being patient. Patience is an outstanding trait to have when overcoming a hardship, so practice, practice, practice. Overcommunicate. If you can't do anything else, effective communication is key when trying to resolve an issue developed from hardship. If someone has wronged you, express this to them in a calm voice and go from there. This could mean you being the bigger person. Allowing yourself to be calm and humble will help in this process. Being kind and sincere should be your approach, and allowing the other person to express themselves will help heal a hurting relationship.

Be there to support and love your family in more than one way. Control your anger and let the other party know that you have been wronged and are hurt as well. If you grew up in a single-parent home, just know that you are not alone. Maybe you didn't have a relationship with your mother or father and feel a void in your heart. Maybe you grew up with a grandparent. Maybe you were in foster care. Maybe you were in a two-parent home with void or neglect of some sort. Either way, just be rest assured that God can fill that void. Let him be your source to overcome. He will open up your heart to heal and get your life back on track. He is a spiritual being that can come into your heart and help you reach that next level of love, joy, and peace. He is love. Trust him. He never fails.

Being in Your Element

When you tap into your gift, are yourself, and overcome hardship, you become stronger each day. This is all a part of becoming the best version of yourself, so you can be your unique you to the full. This strength will help you endure and be at your best when it's time to display and share your gift. If you are a performer, at some point you will be in your element. Being in your element is like being in a zone. It's when you are so consumed with sharing your gift and in the moment that you lose track of time. You are so in tune with your craft that you become unstoppable. You become out of it to a degree of extremeness, so much so that people are amazed and want to know who you are. People begin to talk and want to explore more, especially when you explode or climax. For instance, you may be the next major singer like Whitney Houston and know how to hit those high pitches that send chills down a person's body. People will want to see more of you. They will begin to have an experience like no other. They will begin to know you and know your capabilities. Aim high in your reach while in your element. Give the people something to talk about. Stop at nothing to be your best when sharing your gifts and talents, and let nothing block your blessing of being a blessing to others. I can remember watching my son on stage at his first live performance. He held the mic and began to act as if he had been performing for years. He had no fear. He expressed his lyrics in a way like no other artist that had performed that night. He was full of passion and love for his craft. He was unstoppable. He was in his element, and it showed.

Believing in Yourself

Now that you have uncovered your unique you, it's time to believe in yourself. You have to know that you can do anything you put your mind to. You have to have so much faith in yourself that nothing else matters. You have to dream so big that everyone else will start to see your confidence at an extreme level. You have to give yourself so much confidence and have so much faith in yourself that you even scare yourself. You are amazing, and I know that you have what it takes to soar into greatness if you just believe in yourself. When you think about greatness, I want you to think about yourself. When you think about exceling, just know it's inside of you. You are special, and there's no one else like you. You are created in God's image, which means you are magnificent, and no one can take that away from you. Believe in yourself. Never doubt your ability to live out your dream. Never doubt yourself. You are God's child. You are God's creation, and you should act as such. You were created in his image and likeness, so that makes you remarkable, just like him. You have to have a belief so deep down in your soul that your confidence goes through the roof. You are unique, so believe in yourself.

CHAPTER 2

Defining and Understanding
Your Purpose

Patience is a key element of success.
—Bill Gates

Who are you? Why do you exist? Why are you here? Did you know that your fingerprint is a distinguishing mark that makes you unique?

Before my grandmother passed away, she told me, "If people do what they wanna do, they would be happy." With that being said, I also believe that if you know what God has called you to do and you live out that vision, you will reach your extreme destiny. But wait—that's not all. God has embedded in each one of us a uniqueness that only we have. We were all born for a certain reason. We were placed on this earth to serve a purpose. We are all unique and different and should never underestimate that quality. Never underestimate the power of you. There is only one you. Capitalize on that! As soon as you tap into that, you will go far, and everything you could ever want, you can have.

In order to live out your purpose in life, you have to first know what that is. This approach that I am about to explain is not the only way to explore your purpose. This is just one way that worked for me. So let's define *purpose*. Purpose is the reason for which something is done or why something exists. It is why you were placed on earth. I believe God created each of us for a specific reason, just as he created Adam and Eve for specific reasons. Adam was the first man, and God created him in his own image. Genesis 1:27 says, "So God created mankind in his own image, in the image of God he created them, male and female he created them" (NIV). That says a lot about who he represents and what he is capable of. If you read the book of Genesis in the Bible, it shows all the things God created. That shows you who he is. So, if humans were created in his image, just imagine what we are capable of. If we live our lives for him and work to make him successful, this can bring success to us as well. This brings him great joy. Eve was created as a helper to Adam. Genesis 2:18 says, "The Lord God said, it is not good for the man to be alone. I will make a helper suitable for him" (NIV). She had a purpose as well. People get caught up in living for others, living for money or greed, and living for fame or attention. These are all reasons why we are not happy and live an unfulfilled life. Some even give up things or do certain things that they don't agree with or believe in just because they are focused on the money or pleasing others. When we have a mind-set of wanting to please people and not God, we do not operate in the way that God intended us to. He has a purpose for all of us; we just have to tap into that.

Knowing what you are good at and what your interests are is great as a starting point, but you must go further. When you are only interested in money and fame, that takes away from what you truly can be. If you focus on strengthening your ability in your purpose and your passion, the money and fame will come if that is what you desire.

If you allow yourself to focus on being the best at your God-given purpose, you can soar into all those other things you desire.

For instance, if you want to be a singer, you can focus on singing and strengthening that ability to the full, gaining everything that comes with being a singer, which can lead to receiving accolades, awards, and monetary compensation. Now, let's talk about how to find your purpose.

As a believer, I had to know and understand what God wanted me to do and make sure that I was obedient to his Word. I have found in my own life that knowing your purpose is important, and knowing what you were put on this earth to do helps you live a complete and fulfilled life. This was not an easy task for me, as everyday life challenges came my way.

However, once you can define what it is you want out of life and know what God has purposed you to do, you can live in your purpose. So you may ask, "How do I find my purpose?"

Well, one way to find your purpose is to *pray and ask God*.

Even if you don't have a relationship with him right now, pray and watch God work. Everyone has a calling on their life, and God should be your source when it comes to knowing your purpose. I'm not talking about what someone else has said you should be; that's their particular opinion. No one can tell you what you should be. I'm talking about what God has called you to be. Your parents may have told you to go to college and become a doctor or a lawyer. There is nothing wrong with becoming a doctor or lawyer, but ask yourself, Is this what God has destined for your life? Get alone in a quiet place, go into prayer, and seek guidance and understanding from God to know what it is he wants you to do. Ask him specific questions about why he made you and why you were put on this earth. Always keep in mind that everyone has their own gifts and talents and is special in their own way, as we discussed earlier in chapter 1. If you still don't know what your gift and talents are, reread chapter 1. For me, as I prayed and asked God what my purpose was, I had a session with my coach, and we specifically tackled this together. Yes, I prayed, but I also took it upon myself to do the work on my end to have my breakthrough moment to find out what my purpose is. Prayer does not work alone. You have to also take it upon yourself to take action.

As for my parents, their relationship didn't work out, but my dad did marry someone that has become a bonus mom to me. My bonus mom is someone who I believe is living in her God-given purpose. She spends her time doing things for the Lord and loves it. She is a prime example of someone living in their purpose. She has pastored her own church and been a servant for God in the ministry among many other things for years. She is valued, and I bet God is pleased.

Now, let's talk about how to get an understanding of your purpose. A way to get understanding of your purpose is to *go on a fast*. There are different types of fasts. You can go a day without eating, or you could go a day without social media or television. It's totally up to you, and this is debatable. If you plan to go without eating, please consult your physician first. I am not a doctor, nor do I know your specific situation. So please consult a doctor before attempting a fast that involves not eating. You may also consult your pastor or spiritual leader about which fast works best for you. Trust me; if you want to do a no-food fast, it can get dangerous if you've never done this before. Consult a physician first.

By keeping God first in your life, you are allowing him to be the author of your unique you. You are unique in your own way, and God knows what he made you to be. You may have a desire to be in the medical field or to be in politics. You may want to run for president or be the next major athlete or entertainer.

I challenge you to *pray, fast, and, lastly, read your Bible* to get connected and to stay connected to God and hear when he speaks to you. The Bible is the foundation and blueprint of what God has for our lives. If you read it and stay in constant prayer, you will gain a deeper relationship with God and can achieve great things with a great connection with him. This will help you understand what he wants you to do to fulfill his purpose for your life.

Matthew 6:33 says, "But seek first his kingdom and his righteousness and all the things will be given to you as well" (NIV). If you seek God's kingdom first, everything else you're pursuing will come to pass. That goes for everything, including love, money, food, shelter, you name it. Everything. Don't skip this step. You have to connect with God and know his will for your life, but keep in mind that he loves you and wants the best for you. If your intention is to be a surgeon, seek God's kingdom first and know that everything else you need and desire will be added to your life. I can't stress this enough. You are blessed.

Philippians 4:13 is my favorite scripture. It reads, "I can do all this through Christ who gives me strength" (NIV). You can be all that God has created you to be if you just believe and have faith. You can do anything you believe and put your mind to.

My goal in high school was to go to college and to get a high-paying job in something that I enjoyed doing. So I went to college and majored in computer science. This was something that I thought was interesting and would pay me lots of money, and besides, technology was the thing that was in during that time and as of the writing of this book, and it will continue to be.

My goal in getting my master's degree was to add to what I already had in a bachelor's and make even more money. Plus, I'm big on education and love to learn. While obtaining these degrees, all I could think about was how I wanted to make money and live a comfortable and successful life. I wanted to be all I could be and make a lot of money and not have to worry about being in poverty. I was the first in my immediate family to get a high school diploma, which also made me the first to go to college. My dad and family were overjoyed with my accomplishments.

I lived a portion of my life chasing the dream of a being a computer scientist working for the Department of Defense. Not to say that this wasn't an ideal job. Yes, I did like computers, and I soon realized that I liked to use technology to help make life processes faster and convenient. I love using Facebook and Instagram and other social media platforms and still use them to this day, as of the writing of this book. But I soon realized that this wasn't all God had for me. I knew that he had more. If you want to be a computer specialist, by all means be a computer specialist. But for me, I knew that it wasn't my destiny. It wasn't what I was called to do. I knew that I could work nine to five to have an income, but it wasn't something that made my life full and satisfied. I didn't wake up every morning thinking about working on computers or learning the new software. I was hungry for something more. I wanted to be more than a computer scientist, and I wanted to do something more than just make money.

I realized that I had the wrong focus. It wasn't about making all the money but more about becoming of value so the money would come. Yes, I had a rough childhood and grew up in poverty and wanted to make a lot of money so that I wouldn't have to live that life anymore. But what I had to realize was that what was more important was what I loved to do that gave me life—that gave me a reason for living, God's reasoning for my life. What I didn't know at the time was that if I had just known my purpose and what God wanted for my life, the money would come, along with everything else I desired.

How did I find what I loved to do? Well, while in undergraduate school working on my bachelor's, I became bored and eager to do something to occupy my time. As if I didn't have enough to do with school work already! As I was walking down the hall of one of the buildings on Tennessee State University campus, I noticed a flyer about auditions being held for a play. I thought that would be something interesting to occupy my time, so I went to the audition. I auditioned for a small role because I just wanted to be a part of something to occupy my time and to have something to do. Well, to my excitement, I got cast for the lead role! I was extremely excited and was ready to start rehearsal. This was something that had never happened to me before, and I was looking forward to the opportunity to be the lead character in a play called *A Streetcar Named Desire* by Tennessee Williams. This was the beginning of a new journey for me, and I couldn't wait to get started.

What other way can you find your purpose? Another way to find out your purpose is to *know what things make you happy and bring joy to your life.*

If you are someone like me with multiple things you enjoy doing, this step should be easy. But if you have a few things that pique your interest, that's okay as well. As long as you can list what things bring joy to you, you have a starting point. It's also okay to ask family and friends what things they have noticed that you enjoy doing. They may have noticed you happy when you dance or sing. Maybe your mom remembers your childhood when you showed joy in working out. Have you ever thought about being a personal trainer? Maybe you're your happiest when you're sewing. Take some time and *write out a list of things you enjoy doing that bring happiness to your life*. Some people like to run or write. Others may be interested in watching movies. In your effort to define your purpose, don't get sidetracked by other people's ideas or opinions of what you should be doing. Yes, it's okay to ask their opinion about when they notice you at your happiest, but don't let them decide for you. *Remain on task and stay focused* on personal things that bring joy to your life. Once you come up with your list, *pray* about it. Pray that your list aligns with what God ultimately wants for your life, and ask him to show you what he wants for you. Keep in mind when you pray, you may not get your answer right away. You also may get your answer in different forms. Maybe he will reveal something to you in a conversation with a friend or through reading a post on social media. Only God knows how to communicate with you in a way that he sees fit for you. So don't get frustrated or impatient. Have faith that he will speak to you, and give it time. If you find that you are not hearing from God or he is silent, I challenge you to believe. If there is an ounce of doubt in your heart, it could cause you to miss a word, so be mindful and have faith.

After you have defined your purpose, you need to know why this is something that God wants you to do. With wisdom and knowledge comes understanding. If God has called you to be a doctor, then this must be something that you have the ability to do and are good at, and he will put resources in place to make that happen. Don't just say you want to be a doctor; do the research and learn everything you need to know about becoming a doctor and get your degree in this area. If you don't feel like you're good at your calling, you can always get extra training, pray, let God know, and seek counsel. You don't want to be doing something that doesn't make you happy or fulfilled. Let go of all your doubts and struggles. Think about the great things you're capable of.

Don't just pray. Execute and take action on these steps. Faith without works is dead. James 2:17 says, "In the same way, faith by itself, if it is not accompanied by action, is dead" (NIV). You must *believe, pray, and take action*. We will discuss more about how to take action in chapter 6.

Now that you have clearly defined your purpose and completely understand it based on your prayer and God's consent, you must *set realistic goals and actually achieve those goals* to live a fulfilled life. I'm not saying that you shouldn't have big dreams and huge goals. Yes, by all means, *dream big and have big goals* as well. But within those big goals, have steps to achieve them so you can actually get them done.

During my first two years of undergrad school, I attended Lane College before transferring to Tennessee State University to finish my bachelor's. One of my goals was to be captain of the majorette squad at Lane College. I never told anyone about this. I kept it to myself. I studied the current captain and followed her lead during rehearsals and games. Over the summer, I worked out, fasted, and prayed. The president of the band must have noticed me and my efforts and interest in becoming captain, because once I returned from summer break, he named me captain! To my surprise, he also named me vice president of the band. I was not expecting this and realized that God had not only blessed me with my goal but had also exceeded my expectations. This was not an easy task. It took some work, dedication, and commitment. In the back of my mind, all I could think about was being captain. I loved to dance and loved the way it made me feel. I was also a natural-born leader, so I knew that I already had the character traits to do the job. I just needed to push myself, and right before my eyes, I became what I had envisioned. Because I prayed, fasted, and read the Word of God, I reached my goal! And so can you. If God can do it for me, he can do it for you, but you have to do the work.

Set Specific Goals

If you know anything about SMART goals, you know they are a starting point to setting goals. They are as follows:

S: Specific
M: Measurable
A: Achievable
R: Relevant
T: Time bound

Specific is simple, sensible, and significant. Measurable is meaningful and motivating. Achievable is agreed and attainable. Relevant is reasonable, realistic, resourced, and results based. Time bound is time based, time limited, time/cost limited, timely, and time sensitive. You can use all of these to come up with a desirable goal.

When setting your goals, *be specific* about what you are trying to achieve. For me, finding out I could be an actor and getting cast as the lead in the play in college took some time. But when I became serious about acting, I took classes and went to workshops. I was already a goal setter and loved the idea of setting them, but I didn't know everything and was open and willing to learn more. One of the things I learned was how to set specific goals. For instance, a general goal for an actor could be as follows: "Book an agent."

A specific goal for that same actor's goal is as follows: "I would like to have two auditions, established EPK, postcards to send to CDs, and a flyer by November 11."

Do you see the difference? This was actually one of the goals that I created, and I achieved that goal just as planned. The specific goal gives detailed ways in the process to get an agent, versus just saying that you need to get an agent.

You must also be *focused* on why you want to achieve your goal and what you need to do to get it done. If you are clear on your purpose and you understand why God has called you to do this, then you can start researching others who have the same desire. This is important because it can help you improve in areas and see what others are doing to live out their purpose. It can also help you learn from others' mistakes. I'm not telling you to do the same thing as someone else; I'm saying to learn from the things that they already attempted that didn't work. You can save yourself a lot of time and sometimes money if you take this approach.

For instance, as an actor, I studied other actors just to see their process and how they approached a character. This can be done for anything you have been called to do. If you are a singer, you can study other singers and find out if they write their own music, if they have taken lessons, or if they play instruments. If you are an athlete, you can study other athletes. You can do research on anything in this technology-savvy world that we live in. You can use Google, YouTube, and even Facebook or Instagram to learn tricks of your craft.

Use the person that you are doing research on as a guide to know what to expect in your purpose-driven life and how to live out that life. This is something that will bring complete happiness and joy to your spirit. Keep in mind that people live every day not knowing what they are supposed to be doing. People are lost and don't feel they have a reason to live. The suicide rate is real, and people are lost. Let's *get clear understanding* of what we were placed on earth to do and live a peaceful, happy, joyous, fulfilled life.

You are destined to do great things, and I believe you were put on this earth to share your gifts with others. You just may be that shining light that brings someone out of a dark situation with your presence alone. You may be that motivational speaker who can encourage someone to want to continue living and not commit suicide. You may be the person who comes up with a cure for a life-threatening disease. You may create an invention that changes lives. You never know what you're capable of until you try and put your faith to the test. *Have faith* and put yourself in a position to use your God-given gift and become a success.

Living in Your Purpose Can Bring Success

What is success to you? How do you define success? I have learned that success means something different for everyone. Your gift brings success. When you live in your purpose and what God has called you to do, you honor God, and that alone makes you successful. This is not an easy task, especially if God is calling you to do something that you might be afraid of doing or just don't want to do. Living your purpose brings success because you are living a fulfilled life. You are honoring God by being obedient, and you are making a difference in a world that needs love and peace. Isn't it true that everyone wants to be successful? Think about it. Some may not openly admit it, but we all want the same thing, to be successful. Why do you think people are doing bad things? For attention? To gain something? Success. People want to feel valued and appreciated. They want to feel loved and thought of. They want a chance to be significant. You can have all of that. You can be all that you were created to be. You deserve that. But you must first honor God and commit to your purpose. To succeed is to be successful, and yes, it is in your destiny. Being successful is something that can be planned. If you set goals and work on achieving those goals over a time span, you can reach those goals.

You have to follow through on the rules that are in place to get there, and that will make you successful. By being prepared, you increase your chances of success. Ask other successful people for advice, learn from them, and plan for your success.

Planning for Success

Setting goals leads to success. Proper planning is essential to success as well. You want to take your goals and map them out so that you have proper planning.

While I was a student in undergrad, I became successful. Not because I tried to become successful but because I followed my dreams and was just naturally being me. Yes, that does happen. Even though it is ideal to have a plan, which is what I recommend, there are also instances where you can have success just by being you. What I mean is I had a plan to go to college, focus on my studies, and earn my degree. While attending Lane College, I was named the sophomore class president, captain of the dance team, and member of the track team, all with a 3.9 GPA on a 4.0 scale. I was honored to be posted in the local newspaper. In my eyes, that is being successful. I didn't know that I would be in the newspaper, so I was thrilled.

How do you know that you are successful? You know that you are successful when you have the following package:

- purpose
- vision
- passion
- plan
- discipline
- persistence
- consistency
- positive results

Purpose

My mother used to whoop me for no reason at all. When she would come home from getting high and being out all night, she would take her anger and frustration out on me and my siblings. In my bedroom that I shared with my sister was a bunk bed made out of steel. I remember it very well because it always gave me a cold, hard feeling. I also remember my mother coming in one day and yanking me off the top bunk and spanking me with a belt. As the tears rolled down my face, I couldn't think of the reason why she was angry and why I was being punished, because I hadn't done a single thing.

It was just earlier that my sister, our friend Tiny, and I were singing and dancing to my favorite girl group, SWV. I was holding a hairbrush singing the lead singer, Coco's, part to the song "Weak": "I don't know what it is that you done to me. But it caused me to act in such a crazy way. Whatever it is that you do when you do what you doing. It's a feeling that I want to stay. Cause my heart starts beating triple times, with thoughts of loving you on my mind. I can't figure out just what to do, when the only cure is you. I get so weak in the knees I can hardly speak I lose all control and something takes over me, in the days you look so amazing." You get the picture. I was on cloud nine. It was what I loved to do. Then the door opened unexpectedly, and there she was, my strung-out, drug-addicted, abused mother. As she yanked me from the bunk bed, her forceful arm made me feel the pain she endured. I could tell she was hurting, and so was I. I could tell she needed to take her anger and frustration out, and so did I. But why on me? What did I do? I wondered. *What did I do to deserve this?* I was only having fun and singing. Then I began to cry out "Why? Why me??

As my mother left the room and our friend went home, I lay across the bed and cried myself to sleep.

That excerpt from my one-woman show displays a childhood

experience that led me to create my life-coaching business to help young women who have had a dysfunctional relationship with their mom. It is what I believe I was meant to do—help someone who has had a similar experience with their mother.

Are you living in your purpose? Do you know what it's like to live a full, complete, satisfactory life, full of joy and happiness? I discovered my purpose through the pain I experienced in my dysfunctional relationship with my mother, and I used that pain to help other young women overcome and succeed after being in a dysfunctional relationship with their mom. I believe it is a part of my life's mission to help these women become successful in life, and I will live out that mission until God says differently.

At this point, you should have a clear indication or idea of what your purpose is. If you are still unsure of why you were created, refer to chapter 1. Overall, your purpose will drive you to your vision. It will give you everything you need to map out your life's blueprint. Don't stop applying your purpose in everything you do. For it will open up doors your never knew existed. Also, keep in mind that once you know what your purpose is, you can weed out any distraction or unnecessary thing that could get in your way of being successful. So you will know what things to accept and what to turn down. This will give you clear vision.

Vision

What do you think about when you think of the word *vision*? Something you see, right? Yes. Well, let's define it. Vision is a picture you see in your mind. It is intended to serve as a clear guide for choosing current and future courses of action. So let's think about this. If vision is a guide and a picture that you can see, and it helps in choosing your course of action, this is like a map to your destiny. Get it? You can use your vision to help get to where you want to go in life. Wow. That makes sense. Just think about that. Let me explain even further. With a vision, you now have a clear view of what you want out of life. All you need to do now is come up with a plan to execute it. Bingo! You got it! So what is your vision for your life? Where would you like to be five or ten years from now? What would that picture look like? Can you envision your future full of hope, happiness, and love? Sure you can. Just put your mind to it and know you can do it. Vision comes from the heart. It is something you strongly believe in. It is implemented in your purpose. It flows from your purpose. Vision comes when you see your purpose. If there is something that makes you angry, you can see your purpose. For instance, if it makes you angry to see young women hurting from the neglect of their mothers, then you can see your purpose because it's tied to your anger. Your vision should benefit others. When it comes to your gift, others will be able to follow you because they see your vision and how passionate you are about it, and they will believe in you and your path.

This will make you a leader. Get it? Your passion for your gift makes you a leader, and others will begin to see your vision, and they will support you. Once you have your vision mapped out in your mind, write it down on paper and begin to write out your plan. Vision is like a display of your purpose. It is a clear picture of what you believe in displayed on a screen, so to speak. It is detailed and mapped out to be a blessing to others. Your vision is unique to you. It sets you apart and gives you direction further than what your eyes can see. It makes you rare. It is so distinct that it gives you a solid foundation. I've had vision all along because I knew where I didn't want to go and what I didn't want to do or be. I watched how things were in my childhood and realized that I had to have a different direction in life for a different result.

Passion

As I sat in a room full of judges and critics, I felt the fear that settled in my stomach. Even though I knew I was meant to be in that room, I still had the urge to just leave and give up. But there was something within me that said, "No, this is your destiny." I noticed another young lady enter the room, and she sat beside me. I began to hold a conversation with her to get rid of the jitters, and to my surprise, I found out that she was one of the directors of photography for the film I was auditioning for. She was a kindhearted person who helped me to relax. Then my opportunity came for me to audition for the film. I had no idea what role I was auditioning for until they handed me the script. I did my best and felt confident about my progress. To my surprise, I got the lead role! This was an honor, and I can truly say that getting over my fear and initial jitters helped me! I realized at that moment that this was my passion, and I was willing to do whatever it took to pursue it. I refused to let doubt, fear, or any obstacle stop me from pursing my passion. It was the beginning of a new journey, and I was up to the task.

How can you kill a dead man? If it's engraved in your heart and you will die for it. It. Is. Your. Passion. It is the fire that lights inside of you. It is a burning desire. It is passion. Your passion is inspired by your vision. Once you map out your vision and make it plain by writing it down, know that your passion also serves a purpose. It is the burning desire that gives you drive to push through when you're down—to push through when things get tough. Your passion will allow you to do things that you never knew you were capable of, to the extreme level of execution if and when you discover it. It will give you life to the highest power. It can make you unstoppable. Having a passion for something is so strong that it can be uncontrollable. It is so intense that you can lose track of time. So say, for instance, you are working on a project that you feel very passionate about. Sometimes you can be so passionate that you lose sleep or forget to eat. That's how you know you are living in your passion. It is not intentional; it just happens because of the inner force that drives you to do what you do when you are passionate about something. When you tap into your God-given purpose or gift, your passion will drive you to be successful at it.

Plan

You have to implement your vision and have a plan for your life. It will help you with the direction you're headed in your life. So, once you have discovered your gift, write it down and record your purpose and vision. You want to make sure you have a clear picture of your life's plan. This will help you stay organized and help you reach your destination sooner. Having a plan is like having the foundation for something. So, if you want to be a musician, you need to make sure your plan is aligned with that goal. You could have goals listed within your plan and work on each goal one at a time. Having a plan helps you stay focused and gives you an overall view or concept of what you are trying to accomplish. If you have a project you are working on, you want to establish a plan of action to make sure you complete the project in a timely manner according to your needs. You can set deadlines, and that's one thing a plan will help you with. For instance, if you are an entertainer, you may consider having a plan for your tour dates. You can list which locations you plan to perform at and map out a plan to execute and promote your shows. Having a plan is essential for your growth and success. It is one of the key elements for ensuring success, but you have to be disciplined as well.

Discipline

If you don't have anything else in your life, you need discipline.
Discipline is the practice of training people to obey rules or a code
of behavior. An example of using discipline is when you say you
want to wait to have sex until marriage. You may decide to be
celibate until that time. If you can do this, then you are exercising
discipline. Another example is you may decide that every other
month, you will take meat out of your diet and just eat fruits and
vegetables. If you can do this without giving in, you are exercising
discipline. This can apply to anything you aim to accomplish in
life. Patience plays a role in being disciplined as well. Discovering
who you really are and why you were created is just the beginning.
Give yourself time to take baby steps to accomplish the things you
set out to do. Explore your inner being and be open to embracing
who you really are. Use wisdom to determine how to work in a
way that allows you to be your authentic self. Give yourself time
to adjust to your new way of living and your new journey once
you have found out what you were created to do. You can do it if
you keep in mind what you need to do to maintain discipline at
the forefront of your life and have patience in the process. I know
you can do it. I believe in you, so go for it!

Persistence

While it is important to be disciplined in every area of your
life, you want to be persistent as well for the best results. Being
persistent is key. No one can stop you in this state. This is where
you are determined to get things done. Remember how in middle
school I made myself go to school even though I was sick? Yes, I
was determined. Should I have stayed home? Maybe. The point is
you have to have the drive and willingness to want it so that you
are willing to go all in to get it. This is not easy. Do. Not. Stop.

Keep trying over and over and over until you reach your desired goal or destination. Never give up. Never accept no for an answer. Keep trying and don't stop until you get what you are destined to have. One person who I can truly say exemplifies persistence is my daughter. She will keep asking for something until eventually she gets it, especially in her younger years. I love that about her. She will not accept no for an answer. That is the approach you have to take in life. I remember when she wanted a new sewing machine. She kept saying, "Mom, I'm more advanced now, and my teacher recommends it." We had just bought her current sewing machine and felt that she needed to master it. But she was persistent in stating her case, giving every detailed reasoning as to why she needed this new sewing machine. So guess what? After several no's, she finally got it!

When you're trying to be persistent, you have to know what your wants and desires are up front. Then you want to know what your motivation is. Once you have learned that, you can use that to drive you to continue to ask for what you want, without fear or doubt. You have to constantly push yourself even when you don't feel like it. You should always remember your original intent to help you stay focused and motivated to reach that goal. Once you reach that goal, make it a habit to apply this same strategy for the next goal. This approach applies to actors as well. If you know what your character's original intentions and motivations are, you will know how to become the character, setting yourself aside to just be. Come on, my friend you can do it!

Consistency

Work on maintaining a principle or process to keep focused, keep trying, and never quit. As of the writing of this book, I have a set routine I do every morning. The first thing I do when I wake up is read my daily scripture. Second, I read the full chapter of that scripture. Third, I read my daily devotional, which changes as my need changes. Next, I do something for my business and/or acting career. Then I pray. After I'm done with prayer, I listen to or watch something motivational or inspirational. Then after that, I do a mini workout, shower, then get dressed for my day. I then have breakfast, and that's it. I do this every morning. This works for me, and sometimes I switch it up, depending on my priorities for that season. You have to do what works for you. Maybe you meditate or go for a jog. Whatever it is, do what works for you. Just make sure you are being consistent to ensure you are maintaining a level of satisfaction for your end result. Consistency is important, particularly if you are an entrepreneur. If you have a business with a storefront, you should make every effort to make sure it is open during the hours of operation. If this is a challenge for you, have a backup person to help make sure the store is open during the times posted on the building. This is good for business, and customers will appreciate it. I have seen several businesses closed even though their business hours say they are supposed to be open.

Another reason consistency is important is because it shows that you are responsible. If you show yourself as the same person each time you say you're going to do something, it will show that you are reliable, and that can be appreciated as well. So do your best to maintain a consistent approach to everything you do. This will give you an advantage as you work toward pursuing your extreme destiny. You will become a person of value and will get positive results in the end.

Positive Results

If you have all the above-mentioned traits, you will be on your way to reaching your extreme destiny in being successful! Pay attention to your end results, making sure that they are positive and exemplify what you intended to accomplish to begin with. For instance, when I was younger and attending our family church, my goal at one point was to get perfect attendance. I wanted God to see how serious I was about his mission as a servant. I made every Sunday school, Sunday service, Bible study, and rehearsal for the choir. My dad would give us stars for our attendance and place them on a board in the church. It was exciting to have my name with stars by them, and that kept me motivated to keep coming. The end result was rewarding because I showed God how serious I was about attendance. You want to make sure you are getting positive results when you set out on your mission to achieve your goals. So, if you intend to see the positive results, make sure to measure your progress. If you complete your task and get negative results, go back to the starting point and review your steps to see how you can improve for a better outcome. You can review each step to see where you need to make changes and then implement those changes to get the desired results you need to succeed.

Profession versus Purpose

Congratulations! You have reached a level of success! Now let's talk about profession versus purpose.

Know the difference between a profession and living your purpose. A profession will allow you to be micromanaged in some situations. It will allow you to make a profit. You will provide a service and get paid accordingly. A purpose is living a life where you have the power within to create everything you need from within. Your purpose is what God created you to do. It is the reason for your being. It is why you are who you are. It is your life's work. A profession is something that you do for income, but it is not your life's work. Get it? So you can take your profession and use that income for that job to pay for your dream. I would strongly advise you to not quit your day job right away to pursue your passion. Take a different approach: work your day job and work on your passion when you get off your job. Do what you need to do to tap into your element and fulfill your calling. I'm not saying that you can't quit your day job to pursue your passion. You just have to know when the right time is to do it. Preparation is key. The more prepared you are for your transition to move into your purpose, the better off you will be. So think before acting, have a plan in place, and then execute.

Living in Your Purpose Will Make You a Better Person

When we live in our purpose, it gives us an inner strength that allows us to be all that God called us to be—all that we were created to be and everything we could ever hope for. It improves us as individuals, giving us courage and confidence that maximizes our self-esteem. We all have strengths and weaknesses. If you tap into your purpose, you will find your greatest strength. You will be able to be a better person because of the feeling you will get inside when you live in your purpose. Just imagine all the lives you can touch when you operate in your purpose. There are so many people being misled by certain forces, and they are lost and trying to find their way through life. So many people lack the tools to overcome obstacles and hardships that they have experienced. There are certain organizations that help people find the tools they need to survive in life. Just imagine if you were one of those sources that a person struggling with homelessness could use to get back on their feet. Think about the many lives you may be able to save just by providing a service of positivity while using your gift. For example, if you are a singer, you may just have the song that a sick kid needs to get the confidence to feel a little bit of energy to take a bite of food that the nurse has spent hours trying to get him to eat. You just never know what impact you can make on someone's life if you just operate in your purpose. If you believe you could change a life, it will make your life so much better and allow you to be a better person overall.

Rules of Success

In addition to having the package to be successful, I have created some rules of success to follow as a rule of thumb. There are several other factors that play into being successful, but here are seven that I like to identify with. The first rule of success is to just show up. This was a comment that Octavia Spencer made on one of my Instagram posts. It stuck with me, and I strongly believe if we just show up in the first place, we have accomplished the first goal. The second rule of success is to enjoy what you're doing by having fun. This rule helps eliminate nervousness and fear. So just have fun. The third rule of success is to be driven. If you are driven, you will have a head start in reaching your goal. The fourth rule of success is to face your demons. If you can tackle that challenge, it will help boost your self-confidence, which will increase your chances of success. The fifth rule of success is to be grateful. If you are grateful, your chances of success increase because of your heart. The sixth rule of success is to remain humble. If you can keep a humble spirit, that will eliminate a negative ego. The seventh and last rule of success is to give back and help others. When you help others and give back, you increase your success significantly.

CHAPTER 3

Knowing What You are Passionate About

> When you want to succeed as bad as you
> want to breathe, then you'll be successful.
> —Eric Thomas

Elizabeth searched and searched for a reason to miss the school bus. It was the beginning of the school year at her new school, and she was eager to stay home and finish working on her dream of being a rapper. She had stayed up until five o'clock in the morning in the studio and had not eaten in two days. This was very normal for her, and she had no intention of stopping. She had not seen anyone in two days since she had spent every hour in the studio, working diligently on her new album. She began to play over in her head ways in which she could tell her parents why she wasn't going to school. She thought about saying she missed the bus. Then she thought maybe she could say she needed more time to study for the test—or that she was ill. Either way, she came up with several ways to get out of school, until it hit her. She was in love. In love with her music. In love with the way the song hit when it was played on the many platforms. The way the lyrics rolled off her lips during her live performances. She was pleased with her craft so much that her boyfriend eventually gave up after he didn't hear from her in two weeks.

She thought to herself, *I am going to be the next Nikki Minaj.*

I need to grind and get this album done. School can wait. It will be there, and so will men. As she began to fall asleep in the chair, she realized she had to use the bathroom. She immediately got up and went to the bathroom. She washed her face for what seemed like a decade and became overpowered by a strong force that almost knocked her down. She was so exhausted yet determined to get her album done that she didn't realize the demands of her body had finally caught up with her. She knew she had to pull herself together so she could get back in the studio and finish what she had started. At this point, she would allow nothing to stop her from reaching the top in her industry. She had music books, equipment, and pieces of paper with songs written on them scattered around her bedroom and in the studio. She knew she had overexerted herself because she could barely stand. She was at the point of passing out in her bed when she glimpsed at the clock and realized the school bus had already left. She grabbed a charger out of her bedroom for her cell phone and headed back to the studio to pick up where she had left off. It was the beginning of a dream come true, at least in her eyes.

Have you found anything that you are willing to die for? Is there something in your life that drives you to the point of insanity? What do you do that no one can stop you from doing? What is something that you will stop at nothing to do? What drives you? Do you know what you're passionate about? What lights your fire? What ignites the desire in you to keep going? What's your most meaningful love? I'm not talking about a physical desire; I'm talking about a desire from within that makes you want to give in to everything you could ever dream of.

Having passion for something is equal to having a strong desire for something. When you have a strong desire for something, you will do what's necessary at all costs to get it. Whether it's a strong desire to be a rapper like Elizabeth, or to go to college and learn as much as you can about your area of interest. You will invest time, money, and resources because it is something you have that much desire for. Now you should find time to get rest and sleep so that you can be as productive as you need to be, but in most cases, people who have a passion for something forget to sleep and eat.

How Do You know That You Are Passionate about Something?

When you are living a life similar to Elizabeth's, you know you are passionate about it. If you lose track of time when you are singing, that is your passion. If you wake up and go to bed thinking about something, and it is constantly on your mind throughout the day, you are passionate about it. If you constantly get excited about something at any given time during your day, that's passion. If you are constantly reading or doing research about something, you are passionate about it. When I began to write this book, I realized how passionate I was about it because of the amount of time I spent doing research and writing the content. I was overjoyed with the topic and felt it was highly necessary. I am completely honored to have written this book and hope you are getting a lot out of it. One thing I also learned is that I feel passionate about more than one thing. This next section will explain.

Being Multipassionate

Being multipassionate is when you have more than one thing you have a strong desire for. If you are like me, you are multipassionate. This was one of the challenges I had early on because I am a creative person and I like more than one thing. Being multipassionate, like anything, has its advantages and disadvantages, depending on how you look at it. You can easily get overwhelmed if you try to do too many things that you are passionate about at one time. Through years of dealing with being multipassionate, I have learned to prioritize things in order of high importance to prevent being overwhelmed. I also worked things out so that I could do what I loved but made sure it was in alignment with my purpose. When you are faced with this same challenge, try to find one thing to focus on. Make that one thing the one you like the most out of all your passions. When I found myself in this situation, my college theatre director asked me what I wanted to be known for. So that's something to think about as well. You don't want to miss what's best for you by juggling too many things. Trust me— it will keep you wondering and out of focus, and sometimes you may end up doing nothing. Trust your gut instinct when trying to figure out what you love the most and focus intensely on that. If you're going to be a jack of all trades, try to master at least one.

Driven to Success

Are you driven to success? What do you treasure? What's dear to your heart? These questions will help you explore what your passion is. Once you have found your passion, begin to use that to make your life plan. Your life plan is like an outline of your goals, dreams, and desires. It is made up of what you want to do with your life. It will lead to your success. I am driven to success. I believe in your heart that you have something that you long to do for the rest of your life as well. What is it? Are you in love with the desire to help others? That's also one that I identify with, hence one of the reasons I wrote this book.

Don't let another day go by without knowing what your passion is. Don't let another day go by without knowing what you wake up thinking about and go to bed dreaming of. If your heart is in it and you have a strong desire to pursue it, you may have found your passion. It is something that you will know once you have reached the point of discovery. Dig deep inside and search for the thing that makes you want to do whatever it takes to pursue it, and you will have found your passion. Your passion, like your gift, makes you unstoppable. It opens up doors for you to explore more than average. It will make you stand out in the crowd. If you don't know what you're passionate about, it will be difficult to tap into your extreme destiny. You want to have the drive to do what you strongly desire and be a success. Make room in your life to let God be your source and give him room to show you what you don't know you have in you. You are important, and so is your passion. Don't be afraid to tap into it and allow it to be in the center of living your extreme destiny.

Making God the Priority

Once you have found your passion, make God your priority. Don't get so busy watching others live that you forget what's most important—you and God. Make sure you are keeping God number one in your life. Just because you have found your passion doesn't mean you can forget about or abandon your creator. Keep in mind, when you create a connection with God, that makes him your source for everything when you're in need, so make sure to keep him in mind when making decisions while living your passion. You have nothing to prove to anyone but God, so make sure you have a relationship with him. He has the answers to all of your problems. He already knows what we are going to do before we do it, so be wise in your decision-making. Don't doubt God and don't put him last. Make sure he is first on your list and keep him close. Living your passion is so much more fulfilling when you have God in your corner. He can help you live a life you deserve. We all have times when we may need to pray to him for guidance or for a simple answer to a problem we are experiencing. It's also important to make him a priority and pray even in good times, not only when we are in need. I'm sure he appreciates it when we consider him first in our lives, with everything else to follow. When God is the foundation of your life, that makes you undefeated.

Respect Those Who Came before You

Respect is earned, and you have to have done something to get it. That's why it is important to give due diligence to those who deserve it. Have respect for those who have come before you and who are already doing what you love. I used to tell my son that all the time, until I felt like it sank in, so I am telling you the same thing. Respect those who came before you in whatever you are pursuing.

Never think you are above or below anyone. Everyone makes mistakes. I remember having a conversation with my son about several legendary artists. I had to make sure he understood the importance of acknowledging those who have already done what he is trying to do. So, if you are passionate about writing poetry, you could learn a lesson or two from Maya Angelou. She was very well known and wrote some extraordinary work. If you have a desire to be a hair stylist, you should show some respect for Madam C.J Walker. She played a significant role in the beauty and hair industry. Keep in mind that someday someone will have to show you respect as you pursue your passion and create a legacy for those who follow. You are valuable.

Gaining Respect

There are those who have come before you to whom you must pay respect. You want those who have come before you to take you under their wings and guide you to your destiny, as they have already done what you are preparing to do. Make sure to ask questions and show interest in their path to their extreme destiny. Don't be afraid to be open and honest about your intentions and what you aspire to do. For instance, if you are a dancer and you have a lot of admiration for a more experienced dancer, reach out and connect. Make sure to let the more experienced dancer know that you admire and respect their body of work and would like to connect to learn more. This is the starting point to creating a great relationship. Also make sure that you are at your best so that when it's time to put your gift into action, you will not disappoint. You want to make sure you have something to bring to the table, and I'm sure you will be phenomenal. Be mindful that those who came before you have already done what you are trying to do, so don't act or think that you are better. Show up on time and be ready to work. Follow their instructions and be present and in the moment. This will help you gain the respect you desire. Just be true to yourself and remain humble. Meet and even succeed the requirements of the more experienced dancer so that you appear to be dedicated. Dedication will take you a long way when seeking to gain respect in your craft.

Loving Yourself

As she sat in a hot bubble bath with warm, scented candlelight, she reminisced about her morning massage and her planned pedi and mani. It was all about her. She dedicated the day to pampering herself after all of her hard work in the yard and with the children—not to mention the big project that she had just completed. She was a virtuous woman with ambition and drive, and she loved herself for all that she had accomplished. She was a woman defined, and she lived for taking care of herself after all of her hard work because she deserved it.

While dedication is important when trying to gain respect, it is also important when aiming to love yourself. You deserve everything that God has in store for you. But you also need to have good self-care. Make yourself a priority just like the young lady in the above description. You deserve to have your best life and experience your passion. You are God's child, so you must act accordingly. Love yourself to the highest degree. If that means you have to do some healing or get some coaching, just know you are thought of by others and are a blessing to God. He will never leave or forsake you, and neither should you. Your life has meaning, and you are a plus in his eyes. You should specialize in loving yourself because you deserve it. You deserve all that love you can hold, plus some. Let your love overflow. Speak positivity over your life. Say words of encouragement to yourself and let your affirmations reflect what you believe about yourself. Use words like "I am enough" while saying your affirmations.

Make sure you block any negative thoughts that come to mind while you're on your journey to your extreme destiny. You can do this by preparing your day in advance. If you set some goals for the day and work at least three of them, you can eliminate unnecessary stress and have time to deal with the negativity that comes with that. Say, for instance, you have your three daily goals, and you turn your phone off and spend the first two to three hours in the morning attacking those three goals. That will leave time for you to deal with everything else. Just work on you and accomplishing your goals. This will help you appreciate yourself more through your efforts. Don't slack off on making sure you take care of yourself. Make time to do some things you enjoy doing that take little or no effort. You don't want to have to exert any more energy than you have to. Get a sufficient amount of sleep. Keep your sanity in check. Don't allow lack, laziness, or others to come between you and the time you need to care for yourself. God loves you. Now go love on yourself without regret!

Living Your Passion Makes You Love Yourself

If you found it difficult to love yourself after reading the previous section, keep reading. When you have a strong desire for something, you become a better person by committing to living your passion. You begin to realize how important you are. Work on becoming the best you and not becoming someone else. When you are aligned with God and all that he has for you, you understand that it's okay to put yourself first. Don't let ill feelings, bitterness, or resentfulness come between the love you have for God or for yourself. The more love you have for yourself, the more you can love others truthfully and from the heart. Trust your instincts and know that you are better than average. Love yourself so much that no matter what negative thoughts or doubts anyone has said about you, it will not stop you from being your true self. If someone has called you stupid or has said you will never amount to anything, just know that you are worthy of all that you are and that that person is projecting how they feel about themselves on you, so none of those negative words are true. You are unique in your own way, and you are significant to God, and that's all that matters. Stay clear of people who don't have your best interest at heart and keep the positive, loving, caring, and supportive ones in your circle. When you are living in your passion, you will notice the love you begin to have for yourself. You will begin to appreciate all of your qualities. That strong desire and drive you have for your passion will make you feel a certain way about yourself. You will begin to notice a level of confidence like no other. It is a feeling that will make you love yourself. It will also cause you to love life.

Living Your Passion Makes You Love Life

When you live your passion, you begin to have a different view on life and the qualities of life. Even after you learn to love yourself, you can learn to love life while living your passion. It comes from within. It comes from having love for the creator and all he does. Being grateful and true to yourself and others is very important when living your passion. You have to get out of your way and let God lead your steps every step of the way. You are magnificent and perfect in God's eyes, so don't ever doubt yourself. Hang around people and talk with people who speak positivity over your life; it will take you and them a long way in life. When you are true to your passion and living it to the fullest, you will begin to love life because of how you feel. That same feeling will drive you to love yourself and love your craft, so never neglect your passion, for it will cause you to see things in life differently and have a love for life like no other. Loving your life by living your passion makes you have a different view of life. You begin to accept the things you cannot change and change the things you can control by having a different mind-set. It's all a matter of knowing, understanding, and accepting things for what they really are. You will notice that with this approach, you begin to have more good days than bad.

Die to Self

Die to self to honor God. Die to self to fully become. It is to deny yourself. Surrender your gifts, talents, purpose, and passion to him. Surrender your cares to him and let him lead and guide your path daily. Matthew 16:25 says, "For whoever wants to save their life will lose it, but whoever loses their life for me will find it" (NIV). Dying to self means setting aside our needs and wants in the moment and focusing on loving God and others with all we've got. It is a vital part of humanity. This gets rid of selfishness and self-centeredness. You don't want to be so self-consumed that you forget about your creator and those around you. Let yourself glow but not to the degree of neglecting the most important things in your life. I'm not telling you to forget about all your hard work in discovering your gifts and talents. I'm simply saying not to get so consumed by them that they become your God. Remember God is number one, so keep him first and don't forget about your loved ones in the process. People love you whether you admit it or not. People need you, whether they admit it or not. God needs you. He needs you to operate in what he created you for so that he can reap the benefits, and so will you, if you surrender your all to him and keep him first.

Living Your Passion Can Help You Live Longer

When you think about it, if you are living your passion, it could cause you to live longer. You experience less stress and resentment. Think about this formula:

> living your passion = less stress = fewer headaches
> and less sickness = fewer hospital visits = longer
> life span

As of the writing of this book, this formula has not been proven, but I believe it to be true. Think about when a person is upset and turns to alcohol or drugs to help with the pain. There have been a lot of people with liver problems due to excessive consumption of alcohol, which requires hospitals visits. This could decrease a life span. If someone is constantly stressed due to the fact they are working a job they hate, they could easily develop headaches and pain. Stress causes pain. Sometimes stress has been a cause of high blood pressure, and people turn to alcohol and drugs to fill the void or remove the pain.

When you're not doing what you love, it has an effect on your body. If you are living a fulfilled life and center yourself with positivity, you feel a lot better about yourself and will possibly live longer. When operating in your gift and living your passion, you will have the drive to continue living. Give it a try.

Living Your Passion Gives You Life

Are you stuck in a rut even after reading the previous sections? Do you lack clarity about who you are or about your life in general? Do you feel down at times and wonder how you will get through life? If this describes you, go back and reread the previous chapters. Let's take a moment and think about something. If you have ever felt like your life was incomplete or lacking or missing something, you have experienced something that a lot of people go through. Don't ever feel like you're the only one who has gone through hardship or something that caused you to question your existence. You're not the only one, so don't be so hard on yourself. Give yourself room to grow and enjoy life. Enjoy God's creation. Allow him to lead you and guide you into the path he has set for you. Give up on doubt, discouragement, and unforgiveness. Pour into him and let him use you up so that you can live your passion. Never stop trying to be your best at all you do and give yourself room for improvement in all areas of your life. Living your passion gives you life. It will allow you to be your true self, giving you the opportunity to become who you were meant to be. Stop at nothing to pursue your passion, allow God and others to reap the benefit of your love for your craft, and, whatever you do, don't give up on pursuing your passion.

Living Your Passion Gives Others Hope

There are many people in the world who are lonely and hopeless. Maybe they got laid off from their job. Maybe they were the victim of some crime or scheme. Maybe someone is contemplating suicide and doesn't know where to turn. Or maybe someone is filling a void due to the loss of a loved one. Whatever the case, when people see you living your passion, it gives them hope and assurance that they too can live their passion if they have the motivation, encouragement, and tools to do so, just like you. Never give up on anyone who has had a hard time in life. Keep them uplifted in prayer and watch God make a difference in yours and their life. They are human just like you. They do the essential things in life just like you. Eating and sleeping are things everyone needs to do to survive life. Take it upon yourself to mentor someone or take someone under your wing to help them feel they too can live their passion and have a better quality of life. It only takes a small gesture to help someone in need. You could simply show someone a new dance that you created to make them feel like they too can dance. Put a smile on someone's face while living your passion. I know you can do it.

CHAPTER 4

Finding Your Why and Being an Influence

Never mistake the power of influence.
—Jim Rohn

Know Your Why

This section is important because it will give you your reason for living your extreme destiny. If you know why you are doing a certain thing, when times get tough, it will help you get through it and will help you follow through. When it comes to acting, I find myself wanting to give up occasionally, and it is not a good feeling. Being passionate is having a strong feeling of enthusiasm or excitement for something or about something. Knowing your *why* should have the same effect. I felt strongly about acting once I realized it was something I was meant to do, and I felt even more passionate about my why. My why gave me a reason to keep going. Yes, I took breaks and took time for myself, but I also made an effort to remember my why during those times I felt like giving up.

In life, there will be many obstacles while pursuing your passion. Just take a step further and remember your why. This is one of the most important principles in life. When you have purpose behind your passion, that's also a plus. What others think is not important, but what is important is what you think and how you want to live your life. Knowing your why will open up doors for advancement. It will leave opportunities for you to go further in your drive into living your passion. So get out of neutral and shift into drive! When you know your why, it makes you fierce and unstoppable. It gives you a certain glow. It puts the spotlight on you in ways that no one can take away. When you know your why and live your passion, you can make yourself a force to be reckoned with.

Leadership

Once you have established your gift and know your why, you become a leader. Leadership creates influence. As a leader, you will influence others. Do not manipulate anyone. If you know where you want to go, design your plan to reflect that. We are what we think and believe. Make yourself so valuable that people come to you. You become valuable by being unique and rare. Just think about it. If you stand out, it sets you apart from the norm. You are no longer average. You become of extreme value when you set yourself apart and become more than normal. You are significant. But keep in mind, people will be impressed by your heart. So, with that, you should continue to focus on being all the God created you to be, not what others want you to be. You become a leader once you tap into your gift and excel at it. Others will want to follow; let them, but keep a level head and don't think too highly of yourself. Being a leader comes naturally when you are living in your purpose. When you have drive, it shows, and others will want to see more of what you have to offer. They will be impressed and want to know how they can help you or how you can help them. Having the ability to influence is leadership. People will follow an influencer. Just think about those you admire and look up to who post great content on social media. How do they influence you? What is it about them that draws your attention? The same thing can happen to you when you tap into your gift. You can become a leader while you influence others, so make sure your heart is intact with a genuine motive.

Being an Influence

Once you become successful, you become an influence. Others begin to want to take your advice or follow in your footsteps. Influence is the capacity to have an effect on the character, development, or behavior of someone or something, or the effect itself. If you're going to be an influence, make sure that your actions speak from your words. For instance, if you say you're going to speak at an event, practice what you speak and make sure you are present at the event. If you give others advice about eating healthily, make sure you are eating healthily as well. If you say you're going to be somewhere, be there! If you can't make it, call and communicate that. It's as simple as that, so don't overcomplicate things. If you want to be an influence on others, you have to engage your audience. You can do this in a number of ways, depending on your area of gifting. You can use social media as a way to influence. You can use your knowledge and get it out to those you intend to influence. You have to share your knowledge and make sure you are being sincere in your approach. You don't want to be misleading or have an "I'm gonna get over" attitude. You have to genuinely want to impact others in a positive way. You want to be confident enough to believe in yourself if you're going to have an effect on someone else. Be kind and polite when speaking to others, and have respect for them as well as for yourself. Have an interest in others and their opinions, and keep an open mind about certain topics. For example, if you believe in a certain topic, voice that but be open to any indifference of opinion. Being an influence can apply pressure if you are already well-known in your industry, so if you want to keep the same influence, you must practice what you preach.

Becoming a Person of Value

If you become a person of value, you can be an influence and change the world. Make yourself so valuable that people come to you for advice and ideas, and they want to pay you for them. Ever since I was pregnant with my son, I used to sing to him even while he was rolling around in the womb. I always knew he would be special, but I never knew he would be in the music industry, and I'm sure my singing had something to do with it. I remember all the times people said how cool he was and how he always had his earpiece in, listening to music. Then I became aware that he wanted to be a rapper. One weekend, my son and I went to a music conference. At that conference, we met music professionals in the entertainment industry. We learned a lot about the industry and met several people who could help us learn more about the business side of things. We were also informed about an event the next day that we could go to and connect with DJs and other rap artists, with the hopes of networking and possibly getting his song played on the radio. When we went to the event, my son and I were excited, and he decided he wanted to perform, so I told him to ask and see if they would let him. So he went to the host and asked if he could perform. The host told him that they had a full schedule with no room to add any other performers. My son took it upon himself to sit on the stage next to the DJ booth and talk and joke with the DJ. The next thing I knew, he was talking to the host and still asking if he could perform. Once again, they told him no because the list was full. As it got closer to the end of the event, I told my son that we should leave because they had already told him that he couldn't perform. We had collected enough business cards and had several conversations with other artists. His response was "Mom, I'm performing."

I said, "But they already told you no."

He said once again, "I already sent the DJ my song, Mom. I'm performing."

At that point, I just went and sat down. Next thing I knew, he was greeting the remaining artists as they came on stage to perform, standing on stage behind them during their performance. I was thinking to myself, *What is he doing?* So the last artist had just finished performing, and people were leaving and putting stuff up, except for a few people still hanging around. Then my son told the DJ to play his song, and he grabbed the mic and got on stage with a presence as if he had been performing for years. It was his first performance, and I was blown away. People had their smartphones out and were recording and taking pictures. It was as if he had taken over the world. I wasn't a big fan of rap at the time and didn't really have any desire to listen to any rap music, to be honest, except for what I heard from Tupac, Too Short, and others from my childhood. However, because of my son's efforts and performance, at that moment, I went from someone who didn't listen to rap to a proud fan of my son. His persistence was key to convincing me that he had what it took to be on stage performing, and he did exactly what he needed to do to get on stage. Today, he is a rap artist that goes by the stage name M Sylvic. That represents what I mean when I say to be an influence and a person of value. Because of my son's persistence, determination, and performance, I now listen to M Sylvic and many other talented rap artists that I admire and believe are a positive influence in the industry. M Sylivc's persistence and drive were traits to have when trying to make it in the entertainment industry. I told him that I supported him 10,000 percent, and I have ever since. You can have the same approach with your passion. Not accepting no for an answer was a defining moment for him, and you should let that be your motivation to keep trying in whatever field you're pursuing, even when told a firm no. Don't let anything or anyone stop you from reaching your extreme destiny.

I told my son, "Don't let anyone stop you from living your passion, not even me." Be an example to others who show interest in what you aim to pursue, and strive to make yourself seen even when you are told no. Never accept no for an answer when you're passionate about something, and always go after what you want in life. I teach these same principles to my children; my son and daughter both apply them to their lives, and so can you. My son influenced me to be open-minded and listen to more genres of music. I now use a more open-minded approach in my acting career as well, and I learn from every opportunity that comes my way. This principle can open many doors.

Being an influence in someone's life doesn't mean you have to be perfect. You can strive for perfection, but don't ever feel down because you are not a size 0 model or because you're not tall enough for a certain acting role. Everyone has room to grow and develop, and there is a role for everyone. Don't feel that you must live a certain life to lead others either. A simple smile on your face every day may brighten someone's day. Remaining humble when being recognized can encourage others. When I saw Regina King receive her Emmy for outstanding lead in a limited series for *Seven Seconds*, and I saw her reaction and how humble she was, I was moved. She touched me to the core because she was very happy and overjoyed, but she also remained very humble. This was one moment that gave me hope and happiness as I watched her. Remaining humble and exercising humility in every area of your life, especially while living your passion, shows others how special you are. I would also encourage you to focus on being of value and focus less on making money. If you put yourself in a position where you are valuable to someone and to other people in general, the money will come. People will want to buy whatever you're selling if they feel you can offer something of value to them. A lot of people want to be famous with millions of dollars but don't want to consider the work that comes with that. This was one of the things that was a challenge for me in high school. All I could think about was what field I could go into to make the most money. Money, money, money. That was my thought process. That was my motivation. The first thing that came to my mind at the time was computers, simply because that was what was new and growing at the time. Yes, I've already told you that I like computers and the science behind them. I also like the way computers and technology make life processes much faster. However, I only went to college and majored in computers because I thought I could make a lot of money. Also, keep in mind your mind-set. Your mind-set will determine your approach to things in life and ultimately will be the main factor in your decision-making. My mind-set was on money, and I needed to change that.

As far as what I experienced growing up as a child, I didn't know anything about being of value or knowing what I was passionate about. My only focus was money and taking care of my family. There is nothing wrong with the two, but when you let making money be your motivating factor and forget about who you are and who you were destined to be, you lose out on your purpose in life. Growing up in the projects of Nashville showed me a different view of the world. While in elementary school, I loved to learn in the midst of what was going on at home. I grew up where there was loud music playing all the time, drugs being sold, people being shot at or killed, and lots of arguments and fights. The man I witnessed being shot in broad daylight was running and limping, trying to get away on the sidewalk, right across the street from where I lived.

There were nights when I had a hard time sleeping from hearing helicopters flying overhead or people up and out late at night. I couldn't focus sometimes because of all the distractions, but eventually, I learned how to get my homework done with the noise. It was something I had to do to make good grades, and I was determined that I was going to be somebody. I used my mom as an example of what I didn't want to do when I got older, and I did the opposite of what she did to make better choices. When I got to high school, I did everything I could possibly do to stay active and keep my mind off of the things that were going on in my home—from watching my mom being abused by men to seeing needles lying around the house and being embarrassed of my mom in front of friends.

One day, I had a meeting with my guidance counselor in high school. It was one of the most memorable days of my life. He looked over my school records all the way back to elementary school. I had no idea that he would be able to figure out my living situation just by viewing my school record. After he looked over my record, he looked at me with concern and said, "What's going on? Is your mother on drugs?" I immediately started to cry. As the tears rolled down my face, he handed me my school records. It showed how in elementary school, I failed one grade. I remember failing simply because of missed days because my mother wasn't home to make sure my siblings and I got off to school. It also showed my progress from middle school into high school. Then the best thing happened to me. My guidance counselor said something like, "I am going to help you, and we will get through this." I immediately stopped crying, and a feeling came over me that I had never felt before. It was a feeling of reassurance that I was going to be okay and everything would be all right. From that day forth, he helped me know what I needed to do to apply to college and everything that came with that. I tell you this story not to sadden you or for sympathy but simply to let you know that you can get through a rough situation if you believe you can. Don't think because you have gone through a rough patch that you can't be an influence. If you have a story to tell and you can speak about how you overcame something, you can be an influence. Let your joy of overcoming that situation be your light in someone's life. Let your happiness and strength be the inspiring factor that gives someone else motivation to get through their situation. Even though I had a little help along the way, I was the one who endured the pain of a rough childhood and experienced growing up early on in life. I have a story to tell because I lived it. You, too, can overcome a dark situation if you just believe you can. I'm surprised the Department of Children Services didn't see our living situation, get involved, and have us taken away to live in foster care. As it turns out, that wasn't the case. After my mother got to the point where she was too unstable to take care of us, we had to live with my dad. This was a completely different experience, and I tell you, I'm happy about it. While I progressed through high school, my dad told me that he was so proud of me. I was an influence on my dad because, as I mentioned before, I was the first in my family to graduate high school. This was a big deal, and no one could ever take that away from me or my family. It was an accomplishment, and it felt good. Living with my dad during my high school years kept me grounded because even though my dad only had a GED, he was full of wisdom. I would see him reading a lot and talking about God on a regular basis. He was a minister of the Word of God, and every conversation he had with anyone included him talking about God in some way or another. He made me feel like a queen. He told me I was the prettiest girl in the whole world. I never forgot that, and I kept that in my heart even into adulthood. He treated me like I was a celebrity, as did the rest of my family.

My dad became an influence in my life as I watched him teach the importance of reading your Bible daily. I still read my Bible every day. He was really strict when it came to going to church and loving the Lord, and my grandmother loved the Lord just as much. These were the two people who set the foundation for my growth and development after the hardships I had faced in my younger years. As a result of how he treated me, I became confident and independent. He taught me how to live an independent life, not having to rely on anyone, and also how to be submissive from a biblical point of view. I quickly learned that God was my source and strength in everything I did, and my dad made sure that we went to church for every service we had. He was stern and made sure we did what we were supposed to do. Even though I believe my dad was too strict in making me and my siblings go to church for every service and revival and rehearsal, I also know that he

wanted the best for us. I will say this. As a result of my obedience
to my father and love for God, I have had a relationship with
God ever since, and I believe that relationship keeps me intact.
My father was my influence. I looked up to and admired my dad
because of the example he set. He wasn't drinking, doing drugs,
or living a life of violence or crime. He had a full-time job, and
that wasn't something I saw from people in the projects. Because
of my dad's life, I saw something different. I saw something that
was genuine love, and for once, I felt safe.

God as an Influence

God is my influence. God is my influence simply because he is
perfect. He is the reason why I am still here and can do what I
love. He gave me purpose, and he loves everyone. He doesn't
make mistakes, and he sets the perfect example. We can strive
to be like God and do the many things required to get to that
point, but we will never be God, and we will never be perfect. I
would like for you to take that concept and apply that to your life.
No one can be you. God created you as a unique individual with
unique gifts that only you have. You are special. Even though I
had a rough childhood, things shifted for me when I moved in
with my father and I got a closer relationship with God. It was
then that I knew I was special and that I had what it took to be an
influence in other people's lives. Yes, I wanted to help my family
be in a better situation, and I wanted to make money to be able
to provide for my family, so I came up with what I thought was
best for me at the time and how I could make a lot of money. But
money shouldn't be your only reason for doing something, even
if you had a hard life. This is important because I don't want you
to take this the wrong way. You do need money to provide for you
and your family, but it shouldn't be the motivating factor in all

things. You shouldn't love money, and you shouldn't let money be your God. I had to learn this the hard way.

While in high school, I participated in track, volleyball, business clubs, professional organizations, band, and more. I signed up for a software applications class and ran with the idea of getting into computers because I knew I could make good money. It was all I knew at the time, so I felt that it was the path I wanted to take to help my family. I say this to inform you of the different things you can do to test the waters, but keep in mind, everything isn't for everyone. What worked for me may not work for you. Now, later in my life, I have found my true passion and what I love the most, and I realize it's not about the money. This took a long time for me to find out. It was at that point that I realized that I loved something more than computers, and something came over me that I couldn't explain. It was a feeling that brought me to the point of where I am today. I had a hunger for it every day and still do. I went on to work in computers because I had invested so much time in that degree, and I felt like I needed to use it. It was my thought process at the time, and I didn't have any direction from anyone on how to do this. Remember, I was the first in my family to go to college, so I had to learn my way through. So I encourage you, if you have found your passion, do that! Don't go enroll in a college and study something that is completely against what you love to do. It will save you a lot of heartache in the future. Take it from me and stick to what you know best to be your passion. I hope my example has given you some direction and has created a path of understanding for you.

One of the things I like to do is inspire others to live a complete, whole, and fulfilled life. I'm not telling you not to go to college. I'm telling you, if you plan to go, make sure it's something that you're passionate about. I am now at a point in life, years later, where I have redirected my focus and am now living my passion. I post things on social media to encourage others to do what they love and stop at nothing to do it. People tell me all the time how

I have inspired them and how they love the things I share. I am finally living the life that makes me feel overjoyed and completely fulfilled, and so can you. Your drive should be based on a principle of value and from the heart and a love for your craft. I realized that if you do what you love and focus on being your best self, you're at a great place in your life.

Don't quit your day job to pursue your passion if it means you will be homeless or unable to provide for you and your family. I'm sure you've heard the stories about celebrities who struggled as artists and starved their way through success by living out of their cars or selling important things just to make ends meet. It's good to be passionate about something and living it to the fullest, but if you need to hold down a temporary job to make ends meet until you excel in your passion with profit, do it. I encourage you to live your passion. However, I do not encourage you to be foolish or blind to that fact that you must live and survive life with the responsibility of bills and other expenses. Also, don't forget about your family and loved ones who support you. Don't neglect them to the point where you forget about them and what they mean to you, especially if they support you and your dreams. If they have positively influenced your path to success in any way, tell them thank you and show gratitude and humility. You should have this mind-set for everything you do for the best results possible in your everyday life. These traits can take you a long way when showing appreciation to someone for their love and support. My dad told me that I could be anything I wanted to be and do anything I wanted to do if I put my mind to it. When he told me this, it gave me exactly what I needed to succeed in life.

After I heard those words, I learned to be someone who sets goals and works hard to achieve them. I have taken what my dad taught me and added what many of my role models and mentors have taught me and made myself into who I am today. I am a person of influence, and I believe you can be too if you heed these simple traits.

Another nugget to take with you as we discuss how you can influence someone is to not ever think too highly of yourself, to a point where you think the world centers around you and everything is about you. Yes, you are important, and yes, you are unique, but it's not all about you. No one owes you anything. I would like for you to think about someone you looked up to. Someone who made an impact on your life. Think about what that person said or did to make you take interest. What inspired you about what they said or did? If you can reflect on those things and put yourself in a position to imitate that behavior, you too can be an influence. If we can see ourselves as someone else we look up to, then we can have a different perspective on things and ourselves. I have a lot of admiration for T.D. Jakes and Devon Franklin. I believe they are full of wisdom and knowledge. I also admire Octavia Spencer and believe she is very gifted in what she does. These are people I think are extraordinary. They have influenced me in some way, and you can think of what people have an effect on your life. Once you know who influences you, look them up and learn as much as you can about them. Follow them on social media so you can see what inspires them and see their day-to-day journey and what they have to offer. As a direct reflection of this advice, Devon prayed for me and encouraged me the same way I am encouraging you, so don't ignore this advice if you plan to influence someone.

Being an influence in someone else's life is important because there are so many unhappy people in the world. Just imagine a life you can touch by being an example. You could be the person people feel connected to and can relate to, so they feel comfortable telling you their story to help get through the pain of the memories that left them with a scar. Don't underestimate your value and what you can do simply because of the life you live. A lot of times, we don't recognize our own value because we have been hurt or are too unfamiliar with what our traits are. Maybe you have been in a position of leadership and have led many people just by being you. If you are living in your purpose and being an example of what it is to truly love what you do, you can change a life and, in some cases, save one from living a life of regret.

Too many people work jobs they hate, creating a stressful life that is unfulfilled. They are unmotivated and exhausted. Before you can be an influence in someone else's life, you must make sure you are living your passion so you can set the example. You must not only talk the talk but walk the walk. If you say you are an artist but never take any time to perfect your craft, then how can you influence someone else? If you say you are a lawyer but never practice, then you may want to reconsider or start practicing. I'm a firm believer in being a person of influence, because not only will you impact and change someone's life, but the feeling you get after a person tells you they were moved by your speech or touched by your words leaves you feeling like you have made a difference. Be that way maker or difference in someone's life.

When I was writing this book, I would post inspirational quotes on my personal Facebook and Instagram pages to get people ready for what I had in store for them. I had a few people tell me how they were inspired by my posts. Those comments made me feel so good on the inside that it encouraged me to post many more.

When I did the play called *A Streetcar Named Desire* while in college, we had posters placed on and off campus. There was this little girl from my childhood church that called me up one day; she had seen my poster. She told me that I was her role model and asked my permission to use the poster for a school project. I was delighted and overjoyed that she looked up to me in that manner. It was the greatest feeling that a girl could have and the beginning of one of my most cherished moments of influence.

To this day, my goal is to inspire, impact, and change lives. I believe the more lives that I can impact in living my passion, the more people will actually do the same. I no longer live my life thinking that I should work for money but instead that I should live my passion and let the money come. This thought process took years to develop and was not an overnight thing. I had to do some serious reflection, research, learning, and soul searching just to begin to think this way. I encourage you to not be driven by money but to put yourself in a position of power by living your passion so that you can make the money in the process. When you finally get to a point in your life where you are living your passion and making money, don't underestimate others or think you are higher than anyone else just because you have found your passion and know what you want to do in life. You must exercise humility and gratitude in everything you do. Be grateful for the little things like having food to eat, a place to sleep, and clothes to wear. Don't ever think that, because you have those things, they can't be taken from you.

As I became an adult and worked nine to five in computers, I made what I thought was good money at the time. I lived a life of going to work every day, just like the average person. It became my reality. I learned that this was the norm. There was nothing wrong with this way of living if that's what you want to do; however, it was not fulfilling to me. After I became pregnant with my daughter, I experienced a lot of sickness, and after conceiving her, I became depressed. I ended up losing my mom and grandmother within years. I also had to have my appendix removed. And to add to what I was already dealing with, I gained a lot of weight and lost my job.

It took years for me to realize this, but the fact remains that I wasn't happy or fulfilled. It became clear to me a few years later why my behavior had changed; I learned that I had developed a mental illness. I was devastated. This was the turning point of my life, and I would never be the same. I was diagnosed with schizo-effective disorder, a mental illness where you are out of touch with reality. It is somewhat in the family of bipolar disorder. I was diagnosed in 2011. My life had taken a turn, and I didn't know what to do at that point. I had lost my mom, lost my grandmother, lost my job, and developed this illness that I had to live with for the rest of my life. So I went into prayer and sought God for guidance because that was all I knew to do. I thought to myself, *I no longer have control over my thoughts.* This was really hard for me because I was always someone who had control over how my day went and what things I needed to do to succeed. At the time, I was unbalanced and out of touch. The doctors tried different medicines on me until they finally found something that worked. I had years of relapses prior to them finding the right medicine, partly a result of me having a hard time getting used to taking medicines regularly.

It was a difficult time for me, until they got it right. I had gone through about three hospital stays until I finally got on the right medicine and no longer had relapses. Ever since 2014, I haven't been hospitalized and am living my best life. I have learned to do what I need to do to make my mental health a priority over everything so that I can live my best life. I do have faith in all things, but I also know that I must exercise wisdom when discerning my medical condition. It took me a long time to accept my mental illness and to learn to live with it, but that has not stopped me from living my passion. I don't consider my illness a disability or limiting factor in my life. I believe I am special and am loved, and I know this is just something I must live with. I still am true to living my passion and consider myself blessed to have discovered my passion. Even though I discovered my passion later in life than some, the fact remains that I discovered it. I learn a lot on a regular basis and believe there is value in learning.

It is important to learn more about your passion on a regular basis, especially if it is something that is always changing. The more you know and grow in your purpose, the better off you will be. You don't want to be someone who talks about what they love but doesn't know anything about it or doesn't stay current. For instance, cosmetologists are always learning something new and taking classes to keep their skills current on the latest trends and hairstyles. It is also wise for doctors to stay current on new medicines that could possibly make a difference in whether a patient lives or dies. Dancers should stay current with new dance moves that they could add to their choreography. There are many more careers that have something new that could be learned just to stay current. As an actor, you need to always be learning. That means you should consistently be in workshops or classes, keeping your skills fresh and learning new approaches to acting out a character and with the constant change in technology. It's important to stay current in your passion and know the new trends, especially if you want to influence someone else. You can be an influence on children and/or adults. I grew up loving children and loved to be an influence on them in many ways. Not only was I the choir director at my family-owned church, I was also a leader at almost everything I did. As a role model to others, I think it is extremely important to practice what you preach. If you say you are going to do something, do it and stick to your words. Even to this day, people still come to me asking for my opinion on certain things they think I may be able to help them with. I sincerely enjoy helping others and believe that I get joy out of it. One of the reasons I wrote this book was to spread what I have learned on my journey while pursuing my passion, and I hope that you are taking what you have learned in discovering your passion and living your best life.

As you influence others while living your passion, I encourage you to encourage others to do the same. Just imagine what our world would be like if more people were happy and living a more fulfilled life. I encourage you to keep your head up in all you do and know that you matter, as do the people you are impacting. Don't let the naysayers and doubters keep you down, and don't give up. I know things will get tough from time to time, but keep pushing. When you feel you have reached your breaking point, I suggest you get on your knees and ask God to help push you through. One thing that helps me when I am at a stumbling block is knowing there is someone out there experiencing something worse than me. Not to say that is a good thing, but I am grateful and know it could be worse. You could have a flat tire and should still be thankful that you even have a car, as there is someone who doesn't have that.

You may be discouraged that you got pregnant with a son when you really wanted a daughter. You could be grateful that you were able to have a baby at all, as there are some who haven't been able to get pregnant or conceive. Just think about where you are in your life and know that it could be worse. Also, things do happen for a reason and will eventually pass. Keep your head up and keep moving forward in your purpose as you impact and change someone else's life.

Importance of Being an Influence

The importance of being an influence is the fact that you can be the person to impact, change, or save a life. Too many people are contemplating ending their lives. Too many people don't know what they were placed on this earth to do. With the rise of the divorce rate and the level of unhappiness in the workforce, your example could be the one thing that someone needs to get on the right track. So many are working in careers they despise because they chose a path based on what others wanted for them. Just imagine all the people who went to college and have student loans in a field of study they don't even like. So, if you begin to take the steps mentioned in this book, you, too, can change the direction of your life by living your passion.

Your gift is your key to influence. You have to be knowledgeable in your gift. Stay with one thing long enough until you master it. The more people listen to you, the more influence you will have. If you are unsure of what your gift is at this point in your life, refer back to chapter 1. If you want to become an influence, you must become rare and unique. So, if you specialize in just one thing, that will give you an advantage. My bonus mom would always tell me that I was unique. I believe that you are unique in your own way as well. I remember when I did a speech in high school—the crowd's humbling response to one of the lines I spoke. I didn't realize the impact that I had on them until that point. That gave me a sense of how much power a person can have. When I say power, I'm referring to the influence and impact my words had on the audience, not control. If you want to become an influence, you have to be able to grab the attention of the crowd. You want to make an impact. You want to make a difference. I also remember when I entered an oratorical contest in high school, and the feedback I got from the judges was about how I impacted them and the lasting impression I left on them. They were moved. I was amazed with myself and didn't realize the effect I had on them. I must say I love how I have made others feel just from my words, and I know that you can do the same. So you want to be known for something—just one thing. Don't learn the hard way like I did. You have the key to be known for one thing. Let that one thing be the thing that allows you to influence the world, and watch how your life changes. It's okay to have multiple talents, but focus on one.

Also, another important thing to consider while being an influence is you have to choose your friends and associations wisely. It is said that the five most people you hang around tend to be who you are. So, if you are hanging around people with no vision, you must separate or limit your time with them. Keep in mind that if you are the smartest person in the group, you need to consider getting in a different group. You need to center yourself with people who can add to your life, not take away. Always better yourself. If you are an actor, center yourself around professionals in your community and industry. Stay active in your network. Stay connected to those who are influencing you to continue your growth and development. I tell my children all the time, you should be growing and developing every three to five years. If this means you have to change, then change, as long as it's for the betterment of your growth in a positive manner.

Take the time to look at your closest friends in your circle and evaluate whether or not they are adding or taking away from your growth. If they are taking away from your growth, start migrating into groups with people who can add to your life. Eliminate the negativity and focus on positive influences and friends. Don't invest your time and energy in people who are not positively impacting your life. You are special and deserve the best treatment. Don't allow people to step over you. You are the master of your fate; they are not. This goes back to people who want to control you or tell you what to do. Yes, it's okay to take advice from others, as long as it can cause growth. But if you experience pain as a result of taking someone's advice, just move on because it was not the right advice for you. Learn to be a believer in your self-worth. Know that there will be people who will support you and those who won't and don't care. You have the upper hand when you have your gift to give to the world. You are the beauty society needs. You are amazing, so allow yourself to shine like no other. Be the influence that you want to see in others. Give life where there is darkness. Give love where hate exists. Most importantly, be the change that gives someone the courage to pursue their dream as well and stick to the script.

CHAPTER 5

Sticking to the Script

I have not failed. I've just found ten
thousand ways that won't work.
—Thomas Edison

B eing an influence requires being consistent. You want
to send the right message to your followers. Consider
yourself a leader to those who are trying to find their way.
Your example of love for your passion will show your followers
that they, too, can live a fulfilled life. It all starts with being
persistent and then continuing to do whatever you're doing to the
fullest. Don't say you are an actor and then give up on it because
your spouse, friend, or relative doesn't want you to be one or
because they doubt you. You can't let other people negatively
influence your relationship with your purpose. It's all about
control, willpower, determination, and the ability to say no when
it goes against what you believe in.

You serve a purpose here on earth, and you have values, so
you must commit. Don't let anyone talk you out of them. I don't
care if you are a Jew, Christian, Muslim, or atheist, stand your
ground when it comes to living your purpose. I can't express this
more. You must take control over your life once you know what
you were created to do. It's easy to give in to society and what
your relatives want for you. Yes, some of them do want the best
for you, but in some cases, whether it's family or friends, some
people don't have your best interest at heart or are only thinking

77

of themselves and can't see past that. Not everyone wants the best for you. Some don't want to see you succeed. Some are jealous. There can be several reasons why someone doesn't want to see you succeed. You must find the strength within to look past that and keep pushing. Through your worst days and nights, you have to keep going. Who you spend time with determines your priorities. Also, what you focus on determines your outcome of whatever you are working on. We are where we are today because of the decisions we have made. If you want different results, you have to make different decisions. If your living arrangements are not that good, listen to motivational material in the midst of that and keep pushing until you can change your situation. Whatever you do, keep going.

One day, I found myself in a rut, and I felt like nothing was working for me. I was exhausted from raising my children and got frustrated because I felt like they were not doing what I wanted them to do. I was overwhelmed. I was going through what I call motherhood. Then my children went away for the summer. At first, I was a little down because I started to miss them. But as time passed, I began to feel better. I was getting a lot more done and enjoying myself. Then it hit me. I didn't realize how much I had sacrificed for my children until they were gone. If you are a parent and have experienced this, understand that you must give yourself breaks and breathing room. I'm a person who loves hard, so when it comes to my children, I went overboard, and I soon realized that while they were gone. It's okay to take a break every now and then. Yes, stick to your passion, but don't allow yourself to be overwhelmed by the cares of life. As parents, we sometimes tend to neglect ourselves and focus more on our children. You have to center yourself to a point where you can find some balance.

We have to learn to give ourselves some alone time to take care of us because if we're not together, how can we take care of someone else? In the midst of taking care of yourself, seek guidance and direction when necessary to reach goals you have toward living your passion. When you feel you need more guidance or direction to stay focused in your life, you can watch YouTube videos or spiritual shows on TV. When I was growing up, we didn't have YouTube, and I had to stay in prayer and read my Bible. This is what worked for me. Each person is different and may require a different approach. Meditation may be a great thing to do if you feel the need to, or maybe just listening to some nice jazz music to take your mind off things. I encourage spiritual guidance if you don't have any other outlet or way to listen to positive material at home.

Growing up, I was faced with a lot of dysfunction and instability in the home. It's tough sticking to the script when you are in an environment that is dysfunctional and full of negative noise. As a young child, I was used to hearing gunshots and people arguing and fighting late into the night. That experience left me discouraged and distracted. I felt unstable and lost. I couldn't concentrate on my school work and always felt unsafe. It was something that I went through as a small child, and it was not a good feeling or place to be. In the midst of all the noise, I always found a way to work through it. It wasn't easy and took a lot of strength. By no means am I saying that it was easy. It wasn't. I had a hard time managing. I knew I had to look inside of me and find a way out. I needed a window to look out, so I could see that there was a better life waiting for me. I always had a higher power than myself and just used that to my advantage. I'm not saying this is easy to do during chaos and confusion. I'm simply saying it's possible. I went into a quiet place in my home and started to pray.

Prayer works. As I look back on my life, I realize that stumbling block is over. I no longer have to live that life that I lived in the projects of West Nashville. I didn't allow those distractions to stop me from getting my education. I didn't allow the negative voices in my ears stop me from being a high school graduate, and neither should you. You shouldn't let any obstacle or hardship stop you from reaching your extreme destiny. Open your heart to being still in moments of confusion and give yourself time to focus on what you can during chaos. Another thing to think about when aiming to stick to the script is other people's views on what you're doing and how you're living your life. Don't allow others to stand in the way of your success. If you even think someone is being negative or not supporting you and your dream, limit the time you spend with them or don't spend time with them at all. If it's someone close like a relative, limit the time you spend with them. You may even have to address the issue if it gets to that point. Whatever you do, don't stop living your passion. Center yourself around family and friends who encourage you. You want to be around people who bring out the best in you, not the worst.

My dear friend Marjorie, who I met through her husband while in college, is an example of a positive friend. Her husband and I took classes together, and we ended up working for the same company in the same city. It was a coincidence that I am proud of. I can truly say that we all are lifetime friends. Until this day, I consider them my brother and sister. They support me in whatever I do, even the small things. I have so much admiration for them. They have their own nonprofit business, and just being around them makes me smile. Their example in the way they lead their lives and in their efforts to help others motivates me to want to do the same. Every time we're together, they say something positive, which keeps me in an upbeat positive spirit. This is the impact positive close friends and relatives have on you when you hang around them. That's why it's important to wisely choose who you're going to hang around.

I would encourage you to get some friends who are positive and who encourage and help you grow. You want to be around like-minded people who are not a hindrance to you but an asset. Let the relationship be a win-win. You should be able to help each other grow. You can benefit from the relationship as well as the other way around. This simple approach will take you a long way as you stay consistent in your passion. Be all you are destined to be. Don't compromise or give in to others' perception of what you are supposed to be doing. Keep at it. If you have failed at something, don't beat yourself up. Keep trying until you get it right. When you think about it, if you spend time beating yourself up about a mistake, that's time wasted that could go toward making adjustments for improvement on the issue at hand. Don't downplay yourself. You are awesome! You can do anything you put your mind to! These exact words are the reason why I approach life the way I do. Don't let anyone tell you anything different from what you think of yourself. Don't let anyone tell you that you can't do something, even if it is out of the ordinary.

Enough is enough. When it comes to living your passion to the fullest most extreme ever, don't allow people to get you off track and away from who you are destined to be. It's easy to get in a space where you can get off track. If you make a mistake, learn from it and do your best not to repeat the same mistake. This is an important step when sticking to the script because you want to be consistent while growing in your element. No one is perfect. You can strive for perfection but don't beat yourself up if something doesn't quite turn out the way you had hoped for. Just keep trying and aiming for value in what you do. You want to make yourself valuable to others so that they will appreciate you and what you do and what you stand for. One of the things I do to try to stay current and stick to the script is constantly do research. I also like to read little reminders of the things I like about myself. I keep these little reminders in a notepad. When I'm done reading those reminders, I map out a daily schedule and plan for my day.

I focus on getting my goals checked off for the day, and sometimes if I need a push, I listen to motivational material to give me that extra push I need to get over the hump. Another thing to consider when staying on task is to have such a strong belief in yourself that you quiet any distractions and any noise. If you are so focused on having faith and belief in yourself, you can be unstoppable. First and foremost, don't give up on yourself.

Stay in alignment with what you can do and don't stop doing it. If you get a feeling that you want to give up, immediately stop what you are doing and think about the reason you are passionate about whatever it is you are destined to do. Whenever I get into a place of discouragement, I think about why I decided to be an actor in the first place. I encourage you take the same approach and think about what drew you to your passion. Once you know what that one thing is, keep that to heart and know that will be your driving force to keep you going. For me, I wanted to be an actor because I realized how it made me feel after I played a role. It was a feeling that left me overjoyed and fulfilled.

Carry this approach to heart and stop at nothing to continuously live out your passion. Be persistent. I can't emphasize this enough. *Persistence equals results.* It's important to know yourself and know what your strengths are and how to zoom in on them. Keep track of the things you're strong at so you can empower those strengths even more when necessary.

Don't let people project their fears onto you. A lot of times, people project their fears onto you because they didn't have the courage to do something, or they were afraid or failed at something. There are a number of reasons why people place their fears on you. Don't allow their fears to stop you from becoming who you were destined to be. Stay true to yourself in all you do and expect to change as you grow. Yes, change. Change for the better. Change is good. Become a better you. Expand on what you have accomplished this far. Also, at this point, it is important to maintain your success.

You need someone to keep you grounded. If you don't have someone who can help keep things centered as you work toward the life you are destined to have, hire a life coach or spiritual mentor. If you have someone you can count on to make sure you stay on course, you can do great things in life. You need someone to help you on your journey in staying humble. Don't be defined by anyone around you. Be your own trendsetter. Be fearless. Let no one stop you, not even yourself. You have what it takes to succeed. You have an advantage once you find your passion and can go further in life and up from where you are. If you have meaning behind what you do, you will be valued. You want to keep those close to you who have helped you to stay focused and encouraged and who have helped pave the way for you. Never forget them, as they are exceptional beings who are hard to come by. This will also help you stay grounded and remain humble.

Another rule of thumb is to keep at it. If you are an actor, keep going to auditions and stay in workshops to work on perfecting your craft. You want to keep yourself as polished as possible and remain current. Yes, you will have days when you don't want to do anything. You will have days when you feel like giving up and throwing in the towel. We have all had them; they are a part of life. It's normal. You must find a way to regroup and refocus. If you don't allow these days to be consistent, you will be okay. That goes back to why it is important to have the right people in your life to help you when you get off track. An accountability coach or partner is relevant as well. Take steps to enhance your passion. As an actor, I find myself taking workshops and classes to enhance my craft. It's an investment but well worth it, and your work is a direct reflection of practice. So, if you show up for an audition unprepared, then you know it has something do with how you have been practicing or preparing. It all starts with your approach to living your passion and what choices you make. Everyone is where they are right now in life because of the decisions they have made. I believe if we learn from past mistakes and make better choices as a lesson learned, we end up in a better position.

Aim to grow every day. Do something every day that can help you advance in your purpose. If you are a writer, spend time learning from other writers. As an author, I have taken it upon myself to meet other authors and learn from them. Sometimes a simple meet and greet can help you grow, as networking is an important part of growing. Another person may have already gone through what you're experiencing and may be able to offer advice to help you on your journey.

Don't be afraid to ask for help and support. As my friend Marjorie would say, "A closed mouth won't get fed." If you know you are struggling with something you don't understand, don't be afraid to ask someone who has already done it to help you. Don't be wishy-washy. Have a made-up mind about what you set to do on this earth. It's okay to change your mind if you feel that something isn't working, but don't get caught up in making a habit of going back and forth when making decisions. I think it's important to know what you want out of life, to know who you are and have a plan. If you have these things, you will have what you need to reach your goals. When you do set up your goals and map out an action plan, make sure your goals are specific. You want to read your goals first thing in the morning while starting your day so you can make sure you know what you need to do and work toward that from a fresh start. Then read them again at the end of your day for reflection.

Ignore Haters, Naysayers, Doubters, and Those Who Ignore You

I can remember times when I wanted to feel important and valued. It seemed like the more I craved it, the more I was ignored or rejected. This is not a good feeling. Moreover, if you are using your gift, haters will be there. Those same haters will seek you and support you, and you will be surprised. Isn't that something? But even if they don't support you, don't worry about them. Focus on your gift and go from there. You are important. Forget them. You've got this. What matters most is what you think of yourself. Ignore hate and evil comments. Ignore those who neglect you because they are expressing their insecurities or their lack. It's not about you; it's about them. Ignore those who don't support you. The ones who are truly meant to be in your life will come and support you. Ignore the doubters who put limitations on themselves and put that off on you because of their own fear. Most importantly, when you feel overwhelmed or like it's too much to bear, get on your knees and pray. Ask God to help you overcome the obstacles that are in front of you. You are on your journey to excellence, and these are just stumbling blocks that are to be expected. But if you stay on task and are not hurting anyone through your process, you will overcome. You deserve to be in the position that God has placed you in, to honor him by living in your purpose. Everyone deserves a chance to experience their God-given journey of purpose. Maybe your haters will see your growth and figure out their own path. Who knows? But your focus should be centering yourself on God and his Word. You will go a long way.

Stand firm on your faith and truth and know you matter. Stay focused and keep your eyes on the prize. Don't let the stumbling block get in your way. Just politely step over it or go around. Don't let anyone stop you from reaching your goals. Fear is something that can cause you to lose out on what God has for you. It is nothing more than an obstacle that can block your flow, if you allow it. But you have the authority and power to overcome. You must face those fears first thing and keep going from there, prepared to expect and prevent distractions.

Frustration

There will come a point in time when you will get frustrated. This could be for a number of reasons. If you are a performer, maybe you didn't properly plan your next event and experienced an overlap in scheduling. Or maybe you didn't get sufficient sleep due to noise that occurred during the night. Maybe you have small children that kept you up during the night. Whatever the case may be, just know that this is normal and happens often. The first thing you should do is take a deep breath. Then figure out the source of your frustration. Focus on something else and be grateful for what you have, even the small things. Being grateful will take you a long way. It will open up doors that will allow you to get more, as God sees your willingness to accept your current blessings for what they are. He will fill your cup until it overflows. You can meditate. This can be relaxing and a huge stress reliever. You can also get a massage or take a hot bubble bath with scented candles. Do whatever works for you to relax and relieve the frustration. If you do have small children, plan a day to yourself and get a babysitter for the day so you can get some needed relaxation and time to yourself. Whatever you do, don't allow your frustrations to overpower you. Sometimes I find that people tend to look at the big picture and get frustrated or distracted instead of looking at things one step at a time. For instance, if your goal is to climb a mountain, don't get discouraged by the task itself because of how far you have to climb; work on taking one step at a time until you reach your goal.

Distractions

Anything or anyone that comes between you and your vision is a distraction. A distraction can be a silent dream killer if you allow it and are not careful. It can interrupt your drive for doing what you love. That's one form of distraction. Another form of distraction is disturbances or noise. That's why it's important to get in a quiet place and work. It's normal to have some distractions in life. Try to minimize them as much as possible. Try letting others know when you need alone time and turn off your phone— even if it's just for an hour. You need your undivided attention to work on your craft. Whenever my son needed to work on his songs, I would tell him to put a sign up on the outside door saying that he was busy in the studio. So his sign read "Do not disturb."

Sometimes you may be in a situation where you can't control the distraction, so you have to tune it out. In some cases, you may have to take a break. Taking a break could mean resting for a few hours, getting off of social media for a few days, or turning your phone completely off and getting in a quiet place to work. You want to create a distraction-free environment. Turn off the television. Turn off your phone. Make sure if you have small children, they are somewhere where they are being watched but not in the same general location that you are in. Put yourself in a position where you will not be distracted. For instance, you can lock the door, with a sign on the door similar to my son's, and make sure to let everyone know that you will be working and would like to not be disturbed. You can give them the day and time you will be available again. Set aside certain times on your calendar to work on your craft. This will eliminate any distraction that you anticipate.

Also, it's important to get enough sleep. Depending on the individual, on average you may want to get anywhere between six and eight hours daily. If you have people in your home like children or a spouse, you may want to wake up a few hours earlier and do your work while everyone is asleep. You will be surprised at how much you get done.

Fear

Everyone has dreams, and sometimes you get afraid because others don't support or believe in you, and you may even have doubts about your dreams. People may think you're crazy, and that's okay; don't let anything or anyone intimidate you. How do you address fear? You have to face it head-on. Don't worry about the things you have no control over. Just focus on the things that matter and that you can change. Face your fears head-on and tackle them one by one. Facing your fears helps develop courage.

Facing your fears can help you reach massive success. Focus on the positive. Amazing things happen when you face your fears, simply because it allows you to break through barriers that have blocked you in life. When you don't face your fears, they end up controlling you. The easy way to face your fear is through exposure. If you are constantly in the environment or a situation you're afraid of, you will learn to start embracing it. When you realize that you're not alone and at some point or another everyone has a fear of something, you start embracing it. When you think about it, no one is born afraid. It is something that is learned. When you are a young child, you are not afraid of anything. Fear develops over time, which means it can be unlearned over time as well.

Confrontation

If you're working on a project in a team or are doing a sport that requires you to work with others, you may have to confront others on the team from time to time, and you can't be afraid to do so. This solely depends on the situation. For instance, if you are a basketball or football player, you may have to confront a teammate to let them know when a mistake needs to be corrected for the success of the team. This seems like a simple fix, but sometimes people are afraid to approach a teammate to let them know how to correct a mistake. A lot of things play into that, but you want to focus on the overall goal, which is to make the team victorious by correcting the mistake, especially if you are the captain or team leader. But if you are an actor, you want to have the mind-set that you are your only competition. So the best thing to do is to learn your craft and know where you fit in and how to improve in areas that need improving.

Rejection

Samantha woke up to her alarm clock on a Saturday morning in the city of Los Angeles on a warm and sunny day. As she began to go through her schedule for the day, she realized she had three auditions, a workshop, and a dinner meeting with an old friend from her past. She was looking forward to her dinner meeting but was terrified of her auditions, so she began to run through lines with her roommate. She practiced until she felt comfortable with her script. As she got dressed, she thought to herself, *I am going to knock out these auditions, and I know I'll book at least one.* She grabbed her breakfast sandwich and headed out the door.

When she arrived at her first audition, she noticed that there were at least twenty people waiting for the same role, and one girl had her same body type and hair color. As they called her in to audition for her role, Samantha was full of confidence and just knew she would get the part. After that audition was over, she hurried to her next stop. *Whew, that was easy-peasy,* she thought. Then on to her last audition, and she quietly went over her lines one more time just to be sure. After she had completed all of her auditions, she went to her workshop with complete confidence, knowing she did her absolute best. She was excited about booking at least one of her roles. When the workshop was over, Samantha rushed home to change for her dinner meeting and sped down the street to ensure she would not be late.

When the day finally came to an end, she was exhausted. She went straight to bed upon arriving home and felt very sure about her day. She couldn't wait until the next few days to get her call back. As the days flew by, she realized that she had not received a phone call for her auditions. Not one. Then a week went by. Then two weeks. Samantha was devastated. She began to get depressed and started to have doubts about her acting ability. She then decided that she would get some advice from a talent manager to get some direction and feedback about what she was doing wrong in her auditions. It was the beginning of a different approach and a new goal to become a better actor. She gained her confidence back after her session with the talent manager.

Rejection is when you are dismissed or refused. It's difficult for some, but you have to take it for what it is and learn how you can improve or what you need to work on so you can get the yes you're looking for. In the case of the actor, you are told no or turned down for a role. If and when this happens, you need to accept that it is a part of the industry and is expected. It's just like being a salesperson, as you have to sell your message so many times before you get that sale. Think of it like that. Also, the more auditions you do, the more chance you have of booking one. Don't get discouraged and give up, because if you go just a tad bit further, you may reach that yes. Keep moving forward in your journey, resisting all negative encounters, learning from the best, and constantly building yourself up. One key thing that an actor could do is have something planned like Samantha did so that when the audition is over, you won't have it on your mind. You will have something else to think about. Try it. If that doesn't work, you can take a approach like Samantha's and get advice and feedback from an industry professional. Whatever you do, whether it is acting, dancing, or singing, don't give up. Accept rejection as a part of the deal but don't accept that no as the final say. You have the power to be successful if you just keep trying and believe you can do it. I know you can.

Work

You must understand the concept of work in order to achieve the highest potential for your life. You cannot be lazy and expect to achieve your extreme destiny. When you are in alignment with God, he will speak to you. He will help you discover your potential if you accept it and are willing to receive it. But you must put in your part of the work. Yes, he will do a portion once you have prayed and asked for help. But it is your duty to put in the work. Don't solely rely on God to do all the work. Don't solely rely on prayer. It is a team effort, and like the saying goes, "There is no I in team." If you know that your car is on empty and needs gasoline, don't pray to God to make sure your car makes it home. Go put some gas in your vehicle. It's important to use your better judgment when discerning certain situations. I'm not telling you not to pray, but just use common sense and better judgment before you pray for something that you can solve.

You want to focus on your work ethic to the degree that you are putting in all the effort you need to reach your goals and achieve success. You are God's child. That means you are not weak-minded or lazy. You are highly favored and worth so much more than sitting in front of the television eating chips and watching soap operas. Now there is nothing wrong with doing that from time to time for leisure, but when it is time to work, you have to do just that—work. Come on, you can do it!

Taking Breaks

Now I do know that there are some people who go full force and don't stop until they get the job done. Kudos to them! If that describes you, that is fine. But let's look at it from a different perspective. If you want quality, fresh results, take breaks. Take breaks for the ones you love, to spend time with them. Take breaks for yourself, to make sure you are living a full, satisfying, complete life, so that you can give it your all. Take breaks for the Lord, to give him the glory he deserves for creating you. Allow yourself to get into your element, but do so without creating burnout or overwhelm for you, your body, and your relationships. Let those you love know that they are on your mind and in your thoughts. It's okay to go all in, full force at your craft and complete tasks head-on. But keep in mind that once you have completed that task, it's okay to take a break, unwind, go to the beach, relax, hang with some friends, and catch up on old times. Never lose sight of reality or the things that bring you joy. But a fair warning. Don't take so much of a break that you fail to complete the task. Have faith that you can and will complete your task in a timely manner and don't let fear get in the way of your accomplishment. Rest but don't quit.

Faith over Fear

Fear is when something interferes with God's purpose for your life. You allow that thing to be bigger than God. Fear will stop you from achieving your goals if you don't face it. For instance, I had a fear of learning something new until something within me made me realize that God is my source, and he is the ruler and creator of all. Once I tapped into this knowledge, I felt great and fearless because I knew that I was his child. I have massive power because I am created in his image, and so do you. If and when you tap into your faith, you will realize that you are stronger than fear, and you have dominion over it, so don't let fear overcome you. Your only fear should be of God. Don't allow anyone or anything block you from reaching your extreme destiny and potential. You must tackle fear head-on, stopping at nothing to win. With God, this is possible when you believe. That's why it's important to make sure you are operating in a positive environment, so that you can have success. Faith and fear can't live together. So do it afraid. If people do not tell you that you're crazy, then you are not aiming high enough. Use your faith to distract fear and break into what and who you truly are by allowing yourself to be uncomfortable. Get in the right environment to open up doors that you need to enter to reach your extreme destiny.

Being in the Right Environment

You must maintain a positive environment if you want to excel in living your extreme destiny. You want to minimize or eliminate the time you spend with negative people, especially the naysayers. They do not have your best interests at heart. Keep close to God and learn to hang with people who are like-minded. This will keep you focused when you run into curveballs or things that temporarily get you off track. The reason this is important is because the longer you hang around negative, unsupportive people or people who are doing bad things like committing crimes, the more susceptible you become to doing the same things. Even if you are a strong person, you still could be putting yourself in a negative situation. But if you center yourself around people who have goals and are working toward positivity, you will increase your value and live up to your potential. Center yourself around like-minded people who are tapping into their destiny as well. Work together to achieve your goals. You don't have to do this alone. There are others seeking on this journey just as you are, so don't count them out. Also, keep in mind that you don't want to be in a neighborhood where you are constantly fighting to be safe and are fighting for your life. Yes, there are stories of people who lived a traumatic life as a result of the environment they grew up in and still made it out successfully, and that's okay, but if it is something that you can prevent, do just that and be intentional in your efforts.

Being Intentional

Being intentional in your efforts is a plus. If you know what you want and go after it, you have an advantage. Don't sit back waiting for something or someone to hand it over to you. Being assertive will take you far in life. It is right up there with patience and endurance. Work at your craft with a forward effort, knowing what you want to accomplish without doubt that you can do it. If you say you want to pursue stand-up comedy, work at that and be intentional in your delivery about what factors you want to address. Value your time. Use your time wisely and don't let anyone waste your time. Take breaks from social media from time to time. Give yourself me time where you focus on things that bring you joy and happiness, and you can recoup from all your hard work. Don't compare yourself to others and learn from others. If you follow these steps, you can have a great impact on the world while living your extreme destiny.

Taking Authority

> If you are persistent, you will get it, if
> you are consistent, you will keep it.
> —Harvey MacKay

You're responsible for your happiness. No one else is. Not your parents or your spouse or your friend. You are. Yes, you. If you plan to stick to the script and continue to live out the purpose that God has set for your life, you must take authority over all things that try to come between you and your goal. You are the head and not the tail. You were created in God's image, so that makes you powerful. Don't ever forget that you have dominion, and that gives you authority. There is power in taking authority over what's yours and making sure you stay the course when it comes to living your dreams. Be assertive and initiate decision-making when it comes to deciding what's best for your goal. If you are torn between what decisions to make concerning your purpose, pray for clarity.

So, for instance, you are a dancer and need guidance on whether or not to accept a deal that involves a large sum of money, as you don't know whether or not to take the deal. Get some advice from someone who has experience, consult an entertainment attorney, and make sure to pray before doing all these things. Sometimes you may not need to pray, depending on the circumstance. For example, if you know you want to be an independent artist, and some record label approaches you about joining their label, there is no need to pray for guidance because you already know that you want to be an independent artist. So, yes, prayer is needed, but just be clear on when you need to pray. Take authority over your life and keep praying for things that only God can handle. Know the difference. Imagine all the people on earth who pray to God for things that they can do themselves. Be mindful of your prayer requests and focus on taking charge of the things you have control over, letting no one interfere with what God has for you.

Let's say you had a goal to become a motivational speaker with a similar style as Tony Robbins within the next five years of your life, making a six-figure income focusing on self-development. You have to get so intense that you lose track of time. You have to eliminate all possible distractions, procrastinations, annoyances, and any stumbling block that can get in the way of you reaching this goal. You want to be proactive. Yes, there are things you can do to prevent certain things if you plan ahead. The bottom line is fear nothing, fear no one, and take control of your situation to get the best results you are aiming for. Get extremely, intensely focused on that goal and drill in to make it happen. You can do it. I know you can. Don't be surprised if people underestimate you and your abilities to shine. Ignore them and push through. You've got this.

Overall Success and Perfection

I was watching a food channel with my daughter once, and there was a competition between chefs. It started out with four teams. I will call them team A, team B, team C, and team D. After several dishes had been completed, they were down to just two teams, team A and team B. The final competition had come, and the goal was to see who could bake the best creatively complex cupcakes. I thought it was interesting to watch each team in action. There were previous showings on that same channel breaking down each competitor's strength, and it was obvious that team B was extremely skilled at baking. So as the show progressed, each team had two members. As we watched, we noticed that team A's cupcakes looked good, but the judges didn't think they had the creative spark that the challenge called for, so they were told their cupcakes were just okay. Team B was still working on their cupcakes and hadn't even taken the cupcakes out of the oven because they were trying to make sure that the frosting was just right and made to perfection. They spent a lot of time discussing on how to make sure it had the right consistency in the mixture of ingredients and making sure it wasn't too sweet. The judges disqualified them for not having the finished product. Ultimately, they brought back team A, who lacked the creative component, and crowned them the winner even though team B was known for baking.

This is a perfect example of how aiming for perfection can cause you to lose. Yes, you may be known for something that's your expertise, but if you try to make things perfect instead of working your magic and meeting the requirements, you can lose the battle. Stay clear of the idea of making things perfect. Don't think that specific details have to be perfect or you may not be successful or as successful as someone else. You are the master of your fate, so take control. Don't focus on trying to make everything so perfect that you don't get anything done or don't complete the final task, like team B. It's okay to want to have something done and for it to be the best. You can be the best if you work at it and master your craft, but don't compare and don't aim for perfection. Aim for a quality, originality, and results based on the requirements. This will help in the overall success of your end results.

Focus on what you're working on and not on what someone else is doing. This is another distraction that can block you from reaching your extreme destiny. Feed into those who feed into you. Maximize your faith by prayer, fasting, reading your Bible, and putting it into action! You are God's child, and don't you forget it! Success will come. Do not pursue it; pursue your passion, seek the kingdom, and allow everything else to fall into place, just as the scripture in Matthew 6:33 states. Be patient. Enjoy doing what you love, live in the moment, and live your best life!

Energy

Energy is the strength required for sustained physical or mental activity. It could be positive or negative. You want to surround yourself with positive energy. You want to make sure you have positivity in your life as a direct reflection of who you are and what you represent. You can tell a lot about a person based on the energy they put out. If someone is putting out negative energy in your presence, you want to get away as soon as possible. Focus on energy that's positive so you can get closer to your goal. This is a direct reflection of how a person feels, and you don't want a person with negative energy to interfere or disrupt your positive vibes. Use your gut instinct and better judgment when deciding who to hang out with and who to spend your time with. These are some key factors when pursuing your passion. Also, keep in mind that the people you spend the most time with will have a great impact on you, so make sure they have your best interests at heart. Whatever you do, don't quit.

Don't Quit

There were two men both with the same mission, to find a diamond. They both had their tools to tackle the task at hand and began to dig in the ground to search for their diamond. After about three hours, the man on the right decided to give up because he had no luck and was tired of digging. He peeked at the man on the left and noticed he was still digging with determination to find his diamond. As a matter of fact, the man on the left dug for an additional five hours, only taking breaks for water and to catch his breath. To his surprise, he found his diamond. Just think about all the times you could have been hours or even minutes away from reaching your goal, but instead you quit and gave up. I would like you to take the same approach as the man on the left and keep striving for your goal, because you may be as close as five minutes from reaching that goal if you just hang in there. Don't give up on yourself. Have faith and know that you can reach your goals if you put your mind to it. Just keep going, and whatever you do, don't quit.

Be Professional

When you are operating in your gift, you still want to maintain a sense of professionalism. It will be beneficial to the success of your progress. When networking and connecting with others in your industry, you want to be consistent with your efforts and show respect for those you are trying to connect with. Be on time for meetings and make sure you follow up in a timely manner when necessary. If you know you can't make a meeting, make sure to communicate that. To become a professional, practice gratitude, dress for the occasion, be on time, speak, build up your confidence, and know the business side of things as well. I believe if you put in the effort, you can go far when exercising professionalism.

Have Fun

What is life without having a little fun? If you spend all of your time working, you will eventually experience burnout. If you truly enjoy your craft, you can reap the benefits that go along with it by having some downtime. There are times to push for the goals and make every effort to get things done, but know when to stop and enjoy the benefits of your hard work. It will boost you as you continue to aim higher. So have fun! You've earned it.

CHAPTER 6

Living Your Extreme Destiny

The greatest tragedy in life is not
death, but a life without purpose.
—Dr. Myles Munroe

As Daphne walks on the beach with sand gliding through her toes, she reminisces on all her struggles and things that weighed her down in her earlier years. She is convinced she has overcome so much that God is pleased with her. Then she thinks back to a time when she was tired, scared, and traumatized by all the hurt, pain, and neglect she experienced in her childhood. She remembers the screams coming from her mother's bedroom and how she would look through the bedroom door, as it was cracked, and see things that a young child should not see. It was an eye-opening experience that she never wanted to go through again. So as she walks on the beach, she thinks back to a time when she could not keep her thoughts together and could barely remember things that happened months prior. She remembers all the trials and struggles that life has brought her, and she falls to her knees, closes her eyes, and begins to pray. "Dear heavenly father, please help me. Help me to overcome these hardships and hard times so that I can become all that you desire. I am surrendering myself to you whole and asking for complete covering as I transition into who you want me to be. Let me not disappoint you or bring shame to you, for I honor you and your Word. Keep me safe from all hurt, harm, and danger and cover me with your blood from the top of my head to the soles of my feet. In your name, I pray. Amen." She opens her eyes and sees a little boy with his arms stretched out, reaching for her, saying, "Mommy, Mommy!" She grabs hold of her seed and loves on him like never before. She grabs his hand, and as they walk on the beach, she sings songs of joy and peace to him, using her voice to the fullest and remembering her gift as a singer. She then sees a little girl with pink and green bows in her hair, dancing to an upbeat song coming from an antique radio. She joins in with the little girl and realizes that she is in her element in full force. She continues to dance and grabs both children, then hugs them tightly, for they are her angels sent from heaven in the exact order she had prayed for. A boy first, then a girl. She then remembers that her husband left her a note to be home by six for dinner. So she grabs up the children and hurries home to a nice dinner, with a pink rose and Moscato waiting for her on the table. She quickly feeds the children and gets them off to bed and has a nice dinner with her husband. They talk sweet little nothings until they lose track of time and fall asleep on the sofa watching *The Notebook*. The next morning, she gets up to get the children off to school, and her husband kisses her as he heads off to work. Then it hits her: she has a full day of sessions with her clients and then coffee later with her girlfriends. She has it all—love, fulfillment, family, friends, faith, and purpose. She is living her extreme destiny.

Daphne's idea of living her extreme destiny may not be the ideal dream you imagine for your life, but it is for her. So let's think about what will make your life full and complete. How do you see your life three to five years from now? Will you live debt-free with a dog and a nice home? Will you live a life full of fame and fortune? Will you be a professional basketball player? Or will you be the next A-list actor? It's all up to you and what you believe will give you complete fulfilment and honor God. Now that we got that out of the way, let's talk about how to prepare to live your extreme destiny.

Prepare to Live Your Extreme Destiny

What you do consistently on a daily basis will determine if the lifestyle you desire is for you. Are you waking up checking emails? Are you waking up checking social media? If this describes how you start your day, stop. Let's regroup and get better prepared for your destiny. You want to take steps that align with your ultimate goal. You want to start your day with something that gives way to your purpose and what you are setting out to do with your goals. Create a daily routine that lines up with your goals and vision.

So what's most important to you? Do you want to start with a prayer thanking God for waking you up in the morning? Do you want to meditate? Would you like to have tea and read a morning inspirational piece? It's totally up to you how you start your day. Just make sure it is meaningful and has a base that will allow you to have a positive start to your morning so that the rest of your day can go smoothly and be productive for the most part. This will not be the case for every day, of course, as things happen that are out of our control, but let's pray for more good days than bad. Accept the things you can control and change your viewpoint of things you can't. If you can make a difference by taking control of a situation, then do so. So let's prepare.

You first want to have a clear idea of everything we discussed in the previous chapters. Let's get some goals in place. I would recommend having one-week, one-month, three-month, six-month, one-year, three-year, five-year, and ten-year goals as a starting point. If you want to reach out to a twenty-year goal, that's fine too. But let's start with getting a plan mapped out for your life. Remember to make your SMART goals, as we discussed in chapter 2. Make sure they are specific and written down. This will give you the best results. Do what you have to do so you can do what you want to do. If this means working a day job until you can position yourself to be an entrepreneur or musician, then do so if that is one of your goals. When you take baby steps and complete one goal at a time, you feel a sense of accomplishment and are encouraged to move on to the next goal. Don't try to take a large step all at once. Just take small steps and go from there. Create a blueprint for your life. It will have everything you intend to do for the duration of your life here on earth. Spend time writing out your goals and blueprint, and once you have finished, say a prayer for God to lead you, guide you, and provide resources for your plan to take effect.

Beating the Odds

Accept any hardship you have endured. Maybe you grew up in foster care and never met your biological parents. Maybe you grew up in a single-parent home where the neighborhood was unsafe. Maybe you have some type of disability like blindness, or you have only one arm. In any of these conditions, you must beat the odds. Yes, some people in these situation give up and quit. Don't let that be you because there are others with these backgrounds who didn't quit. Whatever your particular situation, don't leave this earth without fulfilling your dream and living your extreme destiny. You have what it takes embedded within you to reach your goals. Put your focus on being the best version of yourself and living your life to the full, with no excuses. With growth and maturity, I know you can do it if you just believe and follow through without doubt in your abilities.

Growth and Maturity

Just imagine a life where you could get along with everyone in peace. Fewer arguments, only disagreements. Fewer fights and nasty, out-of-hand conversations. When you get to this point in life, you have experienced growth and maturity. Get up in the morning with purpose and power. Take control of your day to get the most out of it. Have a set of goals for each day and map out your plans in advance. Be proactive. When you discover who you are and why you were created, you have to live like no one else. You want to be quick to forgive and slow to anger. Voice your open-minded opinion but hold your tongue when necessary. Don't allow anyone to take you out of your element. Be the peacemaker in times of trouble. If you consider this approach, it will take you a long way in life. Consider change when trying to grow. Change is not an easy task, but it will help enhance your overall value system if you can change in a positive way. When you can be of more value as a person, you become mature. Let me explain. Growth and maturity can create confidence. When you have confidence, you become more valuable, which leads to greater things in life that you are destined for, and God gets the glory. If you let God lead and guide your life, you will more than likely encounter growth and maturity. Once you get a grasp on what you are capable of and fully believe in yourself, you need to have a blueprint of your life.

Your Blueprint

A blueprint is a guide or plan. In this particular area, I am specifically calling your blueprint an outline or plan for your life. You want to include things like this:

- your vision
- your mission
- your goals

You can also add other things as you see fit, but for now, let's just use these three areas to focus on.

Your vison = what you see for your life
Your mission = a specific task for your life
Your goals = things you want to do in life

Your vision will be what you envision for your life. In the last chapter, we discussed vision. If you want to take another peek at that information, feel free. Your mission in life is a statement that says what you plan to do for a specific purpose. Your goals are things you want to accomplish. When writing your life's blueprint, don't be afraid to be open and honest about your dreams and pursuits. Vocalize it clearly and concisely in your plan. Map out what you see for your life, a specific task for your life, and things you want to do in life. These are the elements of your blueprint. You can add other elements to your blueprint as well, like defining your life and adding your purpose, and you can even add some action steps for reaching your goals. You also want to make sure you have a timeline for your goals and follow the SMART goals approach. You can review chapter 2 if you need to revisit the SMART goals. You want to make your blueprint about you—and you alone. After you have completed your blueprint, you must put it into action. It is the foundational information for your life. It will help guide you to your extreme destiny.

Confidence

Become so confident in yourself that no one's opinion or feedback disrupts your groove or flow. Work on yourself more than you work on your craft. Read self-help books and watch motivational videos when necessary. It's important to be at your best so that you can be more productive. Don't be afraid of failing. Take risks and watch your confidence grow. Operating in your gift will help you build self-confidence. Saying affirmations and having a positive outlook on yourself will help boost your confidence as well. Taking care of yourself and taking care of your basic needs are other ways to build up confidence. Challenge yourself to do something that scares you—something you may have a fear of doing. Let that be the first thing you tackle at the beginning of your day. You will be surprised at what that does to your confidence. Overcoming fear is a key factor in boosting self-confidence, and I know you can do it. Face your fears head-on and watch your confidence shoot up the roof! You've got this, and you are on fire. Work like your life depends on it and don't look back. Keep moving forward. I know you can do it!

Burnout

Burnout is a state of emotional, physical, and mental exhaustion. It occurs when you are overworked or overwhelmed. It can cause you to be less productive in several areas of your life. You may experience burnout at some point in your life and wonder how to overcome it and prevent it from happening again. You've gotten to the point where you feel you've done all that you can do and just don't know where to turn. You wonder if you can go on. The short answer is yes you can. Let me explain. You have to take breaks. You have to give yourself space and time to recover and rejuvenate. Even the best of the best go on vacation. Think about it. If you take two years working on films as an actor, you need some downtime to get back to your full potential, or you will go into overload. That's what you don't want to do. So be mindful of your work ethic and of the things you do on a daily basis that could result in burnout.

Extreme Motivation

There are different ways to get yourself motivated and stay motivated. For example, if you run track, you can practice with a headpiece on and listen to some of your favorite empowering, motivating music to give you that extra push you need to keep going. You can have your upbeat, fast-paced music set to play when your alarm goes off first thing in the morning. You can have a motivational message playing first thing in the morning for you while you prepare to operate in your passion. So, if you are an actor playing a role that requires you to be a dancer and you have to train others through your choreography, you can get your motivation from confidence in your body of work by making sure you have rehearsed the dance enough so that you have it down. You can also create eight counts that distinguish each section from the next, ensuring that each count is bold and fits your personality. Make sure you encourage your dancers, especially when they are at their best, but more importantly, do so when they are at their worst when learning your routine. Use your affirmations to build your self-esteem and motivate you as well. Come on! You can do it! You've got this (in my coaching voice)!

Extreme Support

Extreme support comes from within. You have to want it so badly that you are your biggest supporter. You are your extreme support system. You have to believe so deeply in yourself that everyone sees it, and then they began to believe in you too. Expect life to happen. Expect things that are out of your control to happen. Things will never be perfect. We are not perfect. But we can strive for it. You will face obstacles, and challenges will come. You're going to want to quit some days. You're going to feel like giving up. You're going to reach milestones that will bring about change and growth if you allow it. It's all up to you. Only you can make you happy. Don't rely on others to bring success or happiness to your life. It all starts with you and your opinion of yourself. God is your extreme support among your prayer warriors and support team as well.

You can hire a personal trainer that is very vocal and highly encourages your advancement. You can use a coach to push you to your full capability. You can use a mentor or even a close friend who is a straightforward, no-nonsense type and will tell you the truth like it is. Anybody who pushes you and holds you accountable is a good start when looking for your extreme support. Make sure you continue to believe in yourself and don't be hard on yourself, but don't allow yourself to slack either. If that means using a coach, mentor, or personal trainer, do what you have to do. You know yourself better than I do, so put your best foot forward and remember that you can count on yourself, even when no one else does. Take no one for granted and show love and appreciation for all, keeping God as your number one source of strength.

When it is performance time, there is no room to sleep. You have to take action! Choose friends and stay centered on friends and family who believe in your vision and your dreams, for they will be your support team. Your support team can also consist of people who believe in your vision. Get your team together and involved in your progression. Keep them informed of your events and programs. Get them excited to help on your projects. For the most part, they will already be excited if they genuinely support you. Avoid dream killers at all costs. Use your resources to help aid in your development of self to live in your purpose. If you know that you need help, seek out those who have expertise in the areas you need help with. Don't aim to do everything yourself. Cherish your support. When you're in your element, you'll have your support. When you trust God, you'll have your support. When you trust yourself, you'll have your support. When you seek the kingdom first, you'll have your support. When you believe, you'll have your support. Never stop believing in yourself and understand your potential.

Understanding Your Potential

I believe in understanding your potential so that you know how to operate in it. There are certain things you need in order to get a complete understanding of your potential. Here is a list of things you need: patience, discipline, self-control, and courage. You want patience so that you can endure and persevere. You need discipline so that you can withstand obstacles that come your way. You need self-control in order to progress and maintain. You should have the courage to face fears and overcome as well.

Let's break each item down further. Having patience in today's world is very rare with the advancement of technology and those who like to instantly send messages via text or email. It's rare that people make phone calls or meet in person like they used to. A lot of communication is done by Skype, Zoom, Microsoft Teams, or some other innovative technological advancement. Now, as far as discipline is concerned, you want to make sure you have what it takes to be consistent in your approach to your goals and have a set of rules or guidelines you follow to get to your destination. Having a plan will also help in this area. Self-control is something you want to have as well. Self-control is a sign of maturity. If you can gain this trait, you can maintain healthy relationships and friendships. Last but not least is courage. When you eliminate fear of a thing, it helps generate courage if you have what it takes to push through, and I know you do. You've got this.

Knowing Your Intentions

Are you seeking fame? Are you seeking money? Are you seeking attention? What is your motive? What is your intention? Do you want to have bragging rights? Do you want to have expensive cars, clothes, and shoes? What is your agenda? These are some questions you should ask yourself to see where you stand with your intentions, to see what type of heart you have. Knowing this will help you better understand yourself and what you stand for and why you're pursuing your craft. You may already know your intentions, particularly if you have already established your purpose. Some people have a hard time establishing this and may need more time. Either way, make sure your intentions line up with your original purpose. You want to show some consistency in your work ethic and practice what you preach.

Taking Action

Proverbs 20:13 says, "Do not love sleep or you will grow poor; stay awake and you will have food to spare" (NIV). Don't sit around waiting for God to do all the work. Yes, pray, fast, and read your Bible, but put in the work necessary to reach your dreams. God will assist you and guide you, but it is up to you to do the necessary work to make your dreams come true. Get moving. Stop at nothing. Make progress, document your progress, and work to be better the next day. Have your lessons learned and actually learn from those lessons. You're your only competition. When you make your goals, have action items and action steps to follow your goals. For instance, take a look at the below goal mentioned earlier in chapter 2 and how to apply action steps:

Goal: I would like to have two auditions, an established EPK, postcards to send to CDs, and a flyer by November 11.
Action items: Submit to actor's access, create EPK, create postcards and market to casting directors and agents, and create flyer.
You can break the action items down even further. For example, for a one-month goal, you can break it down by weeks.

Action item: Create EPK.
Action steps:

Week 1: Follow guide to creating EPK, add pictures, create announcements, bio, and so on.
Action item: Create postcards to market CD.
Week 2: Get CD list for postcards, create addressee and return labels to CDs.

You can continue this process for the remainder of the month. Now come on and execute!

Now that you have taken action and written out your plan, you are on your way! So let's do this! It's time to actually do the work. Commit to implementing the action steps and doing the work. Come on! You can do it! Keep it up! I'm proud of you!

Now, what did you say? You need money to fund your passion? Wait a minute. There is a way to live your passion without funding. For instance, if you want to be an actor, you could start doing research on other actors. You could use the internet as a way to research one actor every two weeks or every month, whichever you see fit. Did you say you don't have internet access at home? Well, the solution to that problem is using your local library's computer. If you don't have a way to get to the library, you could ask a friend to drive you or ask if you could cook for them and use their computer once a week. You'd be surprised at what friends would do for a hot, home-cooked meal. You can do this. You can do this until you eventually get a job to pay for classes and workshops. Yes, get a job. But just know that jobs suffocate your gift. Yes, you can start out working a job, but in your spare time, work your passion. Don't let your job be your destiny. Utilize it for what it is—to pay your bills and make ends meet. Your passion is for a greater cause! To impact and change the world. To be the difference! To be your unique you! Come on, you got this! Don't let your job be your only source of income. You want to have multiple streams of income, particularly if you're an actor. As an actor, you may need to have a regular survival job and then a side hustle that you can use specifically for your acting needs, like getting headshots and paying your actor's access fees. This applies to any field you go into. Just be mindful to do your best work at your survival job and also do your best in your passion. It will take you a long way.

Maintain Momentum

You want to maintain momentum by using all the above topics and applying them to your life. You also want to keep a daily journal of your day-to-day actions that you complete and revisit them every six months. The purpose of revisiting your journal is to see what areas need improvement and to see what progress you have made. You will learn that certain things can be added to or taken out of your day for better results. You can change up your routine to make it fun and exciting. You can reward yourself when you reach certain milestones as well. So, if your goal was to be a weight of 145 pounds in six months, and you did it in five months, you can reward yourself. Or, if you did it in the six months that you wanted, you can still reward yourself, keeping in mind that if you had done it sooner, you would have exceeded your time frame by a month.

Delegating or outsourcing work is another way to maintain momentum, especially if you are some type of coordinator or event planner. Make the most of your time by being active in every element of your extreme destiny. You can learn to work smart versus working hard. You can do this by finding easier ways to complete tasks. Keep in mind that everything will not always go as planned, and sometimes failure comes.

Failure

Failure is the state or condition of not meeting a desirable objective. It is a part of success. It's something that everyone experiences at some point in their life. No one is perfect. If you are not experiencing some sort of failure, you are not putting in every effort possible to achieve your goals. You want to be aiming for the stars in your craft. If you are experiencing some failures, just know that it is completely normal. Really and truly, there is no failure, only lessons learned when you look at it from that perspective. If you aim to complete your goal by the end of the year and miss it by one month, keep going forward. Don't look back. You are human and will make mistakes. As long as you learn from them, you can advance to a level higher than your current one. Trust and believe that God is the only one full of perfection. Everyone has flaws and things about them that could use some improving. Just take life for what it is. Life. Don't take things so seriously that you become uptight and hard to get along with. Make sure to maintain a positive attitude through trials and tribulations as they come, because that is a part of life. A lot of times, God will test us to see if we will pass. Use your resources to get through the hard times and master your craft to the degree that you expect mistakes and are prepared to recoup from them. Make it your business to be better prepared for anything that comes your way. Learn from failures. Gain wisdom and experience in your efforts to live your extreme destiny. Come on! You can do it!

Setbacks

A setback is a reversal of progress. It is an interruption in the process of making progress. It is a temporary defeat. I believe for each setback is a setup for a major comeback. An example of a setback could be just something as simple as a loss of motivation, especially something that is to be done over a long period of time. For me, a setback took place when I lost my job of almost five years working for the DOD (Department of Defense). I was devastated and learned very quickly that it was a temporary loss that I was not prepared for. As time progressed, I later regained momentum, and once I got another job, I made it my business to prepare in case of another job loss. That's what it takes. I'm happy to say that the transition was not easy, but when you expect and plan for setbacks, it helps you learn to deal with it better. Another example of a setback is when a crisis occurs. It could be a hurricane that causes extreme damage to your home or business or a divorce or separation. Anything that reverses progress is a setback. The best solution to setbacks is preparation.

Preparation

Preparation is the action of being ready or prepared. It is being proactive in being prepared for whatever is to come. For instance, if you know that hurricane season is between the months of June and November, you can do certain things to prepare. Have water and food on hand ahead of time. Depending on how you view things, you may just evacuate in advance to prevent interstate backups or delays. This works out well in the case of bad weather, especially when the meteorologist reports it on the news channels or radio.

In the case of being an actor, you may want to plan ahead for pilot season or even for your headshots to keep them updated as you make changes to your appearance. Making preparations ahead of time cuts out a lot of unnecessary stress. If you know that during the month of May, your sibling gets antic and unfocused, thinking about the loss of a loved one, you can always plan a nice gesture to help them cope with the loss. It may not replace the lost one, but sometimes being prepared makes the situation or transition smoother. Don't hesitate to pray while you're preparing. It helps me get through my day. It just may work for you too. Try it.

Extreme Prayer Life

Maintaining an active prayer life is extremely important. You should plan to pray every day. Pray when things are going well and pray when things are not going so well. Make prayer a priority because it is important. It gives you hope and security in God and your efforts, knowing that you are seeking help or thanking him. It builds confidence in whatever you're praying for. If you pray about everything before making decisions, particularly major decisions, you will make more informed choices. I believe that everything happens for a reason, and just like the actor Monique Coleman once said, "What's for you cannot pass you." Think about it. When you are in doubt about something, particularly your purpose, fall to your knees and pray to God. When you are at odds about a major career decision, stop what you are doing and pray. Pray consistently, pray regularly, and pray just because. To make your prayer life extreme, just make sure you are humble, grateful, and consistent with your prayer request and have a genuine connection with God. This will bring you extreme success.

Extreme Success

What is extreme success to you? Extreme success is when you have accomplished everything you want out of life, but there is still more to accomplish, and you are willing to do what it takes to accomplish it. You can obtain extreme success on a deeper level by hiring a coach. Also, keep in mind not to chase success. Work on yourself. Work on becoming more valuable to the point where people will want to hire you and you don't have to look for a job. There are several things you can do to become valuable. Learn a new language. Learn to be more open-minded, allowing yourself to be objective and open to hearing someone else's opinion. You can invest in training in your area or particular field of interest. You can practice your craft, especially if you are a singer or artist. You can work on your vocals or even hire a specialist to help you with vocal lessons. If you are an artist, you can take classes and develop more techniques. Whatever you do, don't stop learning and growing and developing yourself more and more into the person God has planned you to be. When you become so valuable that others start asking for your opinion and offer to pay you, with God in your corner, you have reached extreme success. But don't stop there. Keep aiming high. You've got this.

Releasing Pressure

Don't try to live up to others' expectations of you; only honor God's expectations. He is your go-to for everything, and therefore he will release any pressure you experience on your journey to living your extreme destiny. Only take on what you can handle. Don't try to overdo things. Keep a simple approach to attacking tasks and use preventive measures to help release pressure. If you are an organizer, tackle one project at a time. Limit the amount of interruptions and distractions. You can do this by making sure you're in a quiet place where no one will interrupt you. You can also let others know in advance that you will need your privacy. Exercise is another way to release pressure. If you can find time to work out a few times a week, it could help. Let the past be just that, the past. Have your lessons learned and move forward.

Looking in the Mirror

If you take a step back and look in the mirror, there is no one to blame for your success but you. If you look into that same mirror, there is no one to blame for your failures but you. Life is a lesson. When you understand that you are the one who makes your dreams come true, you will go far. It's all up to you. Don't point fingers or blame anyone for your faults or lack. I can remember a time when I blamed everyone for my mistakes and lack of success. I pointed fingers at my mom, dad, grandmother, ex-spouse, you name it. I was dead wrong. It wasn't about them at all. The decisions that I made came from me, and I had to own up to it. Every decision you make today will impact where you will be five years from now. Take ownership of your failures and successes. They go hand in hand. Focus on learning and educating yourself on how to make improvements in your life. You don't have to have a college education to be successful, even though it doesn't hurt to have one. There are several ways to educate yourself. Find ways to be informed in your area of expertise and work on honing the necessary skill set to better yourself. I know you can do this. You can count on you.

Maintaining

Focus. Maintain focus. Refocus. Exercise discipline. Be persistent. Be consistent. Persevere. All of these things will help you maintain in your gifting. If you are an actor, it's easy to lose focus when you are told no often. You get discouraged and begin to lose sight of your why and your original goal. When you start to feel like this, you have to regain focus and remember why you chose to be an actor in the first place, so that you can get back on track. I know this is not an easy step, and this is something that I have experienced, so I know firsthand what you may be experiencing. You want to trust your gut instinct to know that you're destined for greatness and exercise self-discipline to maintain. That could mean continuing to stay in classes to make sure you're constantly developing yourself into the actor you want to become. It may mean consistently doing those things that give you results. Whatever you do, don't stop.

Acceptance

There will come a point in life when you have to accept that not everyone will like you. It's important to understand this so that it is not a defining factor in your decision-making. For instance, don't let someone else's opinion of volleyball stop you from becoming a volleyball player. This applies to any sport, gift, or passion you may have. Don't worry what others think. You are a child of God. He is your source, and he is the reason you will reign in whatever area you choose to go with. Whether it be a professional basketball player, a gymnast, singer, dancer, doctor, or special ed teacher, you will rule! Philippians 4:5–7 says, "Do not be anxious about anything, but in every situation, by prayer and petition, with thanksgiving, present your requests to God. And the peace of God, which transcends all understanding, will guard your hearts and your minds in Christ Jesus" (NIV). Stress is a big part of what you will experience if you don't learn to manage your time. Remember, you can't please everyone. Educate yourself, take a break, and keep in mind that God is your source in everything you do. Being proactive is another way to prevent stress. If you can plan out your day, it will help eliminate any unnecessary stress and will impact your performance.

Extreme Performance

Your value attracts wealth. Become a person of value through your work. The magnitude with which you perform is solely up to you and your desire and willpower to ignite the fire within. It is your destiny to have extreme performance in your efforts while pursing your passion. It's all up to you. You can wake up in the morning with a positive attitude, or you can wake up with a negative attitude. It all starts with you and your drive. There are a few things to consider when seeking extreme performance.

First, you must have the willpower to want it. It has to be buried in your heart, and you must release it like never before. Second, you must research. You have to know enough about your craft to execute it to the max. So, if you are a rapper, you must study the history and be familiar with other rap artists. Third, you must have discipline. Discipline is the essential element to getting what you want. It will allow you to be consistent and focused. It brings out all the necessary tools you need to get the job done. It pushes the issue. Fourth, you must nourish your relationships and love on those who have supported you. This includes family, friends, and fans. Never forget about those who have been in your corner in some shape or form. It could have been a nice phone call or just a gesture that said, "You've got this" or "Keep pushing." Fifth, you want to be in good health. In order to live out your vision, you need to be alive, right? Exactly. So make an honest effort to take care of your body, whether it be proper nutrition or exercise and enough sleep. Make it a requirement. Sixth, network. Get out and meet new, interesting people. Collect business cards, and lastly, learn something new. Make it your business to step out of your comfort zone. You'll be glad you did. Now max out to fulfill your passion and live your extreme destiny!

CHAPTER 7

Passion Fulfilled: What's Next?

> Life has no limitations, except
> the ones you make.
> —Les Brown

He woke up to the sun beaming through his blinds. He had left them open after a night full of fun and a heartfelt performance that left him completely satisfied with the outcome. So many people were present. He had a full team with everyone there and a fan base like no other. It was a maximum success like no other, and to top it all off, the support, love, and energy of his family and friends proved that he had made it. It took fifteen years for him to reach this level of success, and he couldn't believe that God had spoken this outcome to him at such a young age, and he stuck to his word by believing in him and making him whole and complete. As he woke up from his peaceful sleep, he began to pray, and then he realized that he was completely satisfied and fulfilled with his life at that point. He also felt that he had nowhere to go from there and needed direction, so he prayed and asked God what he wanted him to do, and I believe the Lord gave him direction.

Is your passion ever really fulfilled?

We've talked about gifts, talents, dreams, goals, and how to take action. Now you should be executing your plan to live your passion and your extreme destiny. Yes! This should be a relieving, great feeling. At this point, you're probably wondering what to do now that you have accomplished all of this; you know who you are and what you're supposed to be doing. Maybe you're like the guy who woke up with the sun beaming through the blinds, and need to know what to do next and want to have a conversation with God. If that is you, don't be afraid to ask him for your next move or to even ask for guidance on what he wants you to do next. Whatever you do, don't stop there.

Now that you have exceled and are living your best life, what's next?

After I completed my college degrees, I still wanted more. There is a difference between being greedy and just wanting to live your best life. My desire was hunger for more of what I already had in my life and to help as many people as possible—which is why I'm sharing this information with you in this book. Yes, I had my degrees, I worked my job, but I soon realized that it wasn't all God had for me. I knew that he had more. I knew I had more inside of me. So what did I do? I kept going. Keep going. Isn't this what God would want us to do? Never stop when you get to the end. Keep going into a new beginning where there is no end. You can go even further. The sky is beyond the limit. You are as good as you allow yourself to be. When you think you've reached the end, there's always room for more, so don't stop there. Keep pushing. Explore. Always know that you are never too old to live your best life. Believe. It's never too late. Believe in yourself, and others will believe in you too. Allow yourself to make mistakes and learn from them. Just know that failure is a part of success. No one is perfect, but you are perfect in God's eyes.

You are your only competition. Focus on becoming better than you last were. If you are an artist, focus on making your next piece of work better than your last and keep doing this after each piece. That goes for actual artwork or for a performing artist. That goes for each performance, making sure to advance on each performance, improving your overall body of work to the next level of excellence. Maximize your belief system in yourself and invest in your self-development. Read self-help and self-development books. Listen to motivational podcasts and get feedback on your progress from the experts, like your mentors and coaches.

Always work on becoming better at your craft. Don't compare yourself to others and don't compete with others. Keep in mind your present level of success and what that means to you. You can expand on that and further your expectations of yourself. Yes, I know, you heard all this before in the previous chapters. I get it. So why am I telling you this information again? To keep you motivated! Yes, you! You are your greatest asset, as well as your gift, so maximize that. In your findings, you will see that you can reach an extreme level of satisfaction, only if you continue to thrive and believe in yourself as I believe in you. You can fulfill your purpose if you can see beyond your current level of success and create more for yourself. Increase your progress by gaining more and constantly investing in yourself. You are important, so treat yourself like so. You can do better than your best if you stay focused and keep at it. Don't accept anything that blocks all that you were created to be. You deserve extreme happiness, but you have to continuously put in the work. Don't live in the past. You have to overcome and move on from your previous accomplishment and create new ones if you want to live your extreme destiny. A lot of times, a crisis will occur and cause you to get out of your comfort zone and use abilities you didn't know you had. In certain situations or crises, you learn something new and better about yourself. So keep that in mind when you are trying to maximize your potential and become extremely successful.

You must also continue to have a relationship with God in order to live your extreme destiny. Even if you fall off track, you can always reconnect with him and watch how things begin to fall into place. God is the source for your creation and the being that gave you purpose for life, so don't take that lightly. He knows and understands you and your needs. Direct all of your cares and fears to him, and he will show you the way. Keep in mind that it takes faith to continue to believe in God and consistently follow him. He is your creator, so everything you do must please him. He is the one who will give you everything you need and desire if you stay in faith and seek his kingdom.

Success without a complete understanding of God's purpose for your life doesn't hold substance for your life. You want to make sure you completely understand why God created you and the meaning of your life before you can live out your potential. So make sure you follow the guidelines of the previous chapters to find your purpose.

You want to maintain a relationship with God so you have complete confidence in him and in yourself. Just imagine waking up happy, fulfilled, and loved, knowing how to start your day and what to do every day. Just imagine having a purpose-driven life with meaning and substance. Can you see yourself grinding to make God happy and being successful in the process? Can you feel the wholeness and complete satisfaction of your being?

These are some things to consider when you are on your journey to continuously having and maintaining a relationship with God. This relationship is the key to all your desires and needs, so keep him first and watch your life change for the better, and others will see you in a different light. God will be in your corner through every obstacle and every hurdle that stands in your way, but I know you can excel and succeed in all you do, if you just keep the faith and relationship with him. Another thing to consider while living your life to the full is to complete tasks. Just because you start something doesn't mean you are going to finish it. You want to follow all the way through and complete your tasks to continue to gain momentum to help you stay the course. We must stay the course regardless of hardships, discouragement, and anything that can get in the way. The only way to overcome is to continue to work at it one step at a time. Some things that can block or hinder your growth in reaching your extreme destiny are your enemies. Know your enemies and defeat them. This is a challenge, but I know you can do it. Your enemies are those things that get in the way of your progress. They are things like fear, sin, lack, procrastination, and disobedience.

Fear, as discussed in chapter 5, should only be a fear of God. He is your source to overcome all obstacles and challenges. Let your faith neutralize your drive to overcome fear. Sin is when you intentionally or unintentionally rebel against God. Pray, ask God for forgiveness, and keep it moving. You cannot truly know and connect with God if you are at odds with him due to sin. Lack can be from a scarcity mind-set and limiting beliefs. Procrastination is when you delay something and usually stems from some form of discouragement. Disobedience blocks God's blessing for your life and leads to things that can stop the progress of your success.

Some mistakes can block your blessings as well. Even if you have had past failures or mistakes, don't get stuck. Keep pushing and recoup. Distractions will come and will require self-discipline. If you can take on a task one step at a time in small pieces on a daily basis, you can gain discipline until you eventually reach your goal of continued success.

Creating Continued Success

You want to position yourself where you can create continued success. You want to excel to a degree of exceptionalism, to the point where you are admired and looked up to. Create continued success by gaining knowledge, wisdom, and continued understanding of your passion and purpose. Take authority and tackle all obstacles, and let nothing and no one stop you from pushing through the hard times. Pinpoint areas of strength and magnify them more and more. You are the solution to some problem. Determine what that problem is and do your magic. You are awesome! Be real. Be authentic. Be you. Always be yourself in all situations, letting no one control your originality and who God created you to be. If you continue to be connected to God and connected to your inner self, you can have continued success. Be true to who you are, allowing nothing but love and support of others to give you the extra push you need to continue on your road to living your extreme destiny.

Breaking the Rules

When is it okay to break the rules? It's okay to break the rules when you have established a certain level of success. Don't be afraid to step outside the box. Don't be afraid to be different. Dare to be different. How do you break the rules? By not worrying about anyone else's opinion of you. Granted, before you start breaking rules, there are foundational rules you must follow to get your foot in the door, especially as an actor. For instance, you will need a headshot and résumé to get started. Once you have made a name for yourself, you can pretty much do what you want to do as long as you are not doing anything illegal or hurting anyone.

How to Sustain

The field you are in will determine how you will be able to sustain. If you are an actor starting out, you will need to have a survival job. If you are a runner, you will need to learn an extreme work ethic and practice to get the desired results on the track. Work is an essential part of growth. It will put you ahead. Start your day early. Just start. In order to sustain at the desired level, you want to be proactive. For instance, if you are an entertainer with a performance in December, get an early start in preparation in the months prior. Make one move at a time. Focus on baby steps and putting one foot in front of the other. Make sacrifices. Spend time with your loved ones and make time for the important things. Then get back to work. Love what you do and be fearless and relentless.

Lessons Learned

Leave your past mistakes in the past. Learn from your mistakes and work on improving and not repeating the same mistakes again. Trust yourself to do this. It will not be easy, but it is doable. You just have to learn from the things that didn't work out. For instance, if you are a professional athlete and your team lost the game, you can review the footage from your game and pinpoint the plays that need work. A lot of football players use these technique when reviewing plays to learn from other players and learn their strategy as well. Just remember to learn from your previous mistakes and work on improving them. One thing I used to do when I was a dancer in college was get feedback from alumni about our performances. As I was the dance choreographer, it meant a lot to me to hear the alumni say that we did a good job. That's when I knew that my approach to choreography worked, so I continued to implement the same strategy. Don't dwell on your mistakes and mishaps; learn from them and keep it moving. If something isn't broke, don't fix it. You can do this!

Being Original

This is very important if you are a singer or dance choreographer. If you are a singer that writes your own material, when writing your materials, focus on your originality and being you. Let your lyrics stand for something, with meaning. Focus on being authentic and make sure to use your creativity to the full. If you are dance choreographer, try to make your dance routine as original as possible. You can even come up with a new dance like several other entertainers have done. Let it be unique to you so that others can see the originality as well. Believe in yourself and keep your head up in whatever field or areas you specialize in. Also, keep in mind that you have the same amount of time in the day just as anyone, so use it wisely. Time is of the essence, so you don't want to waste it on nonsense. Have respect for your time and know the importance of being original. This is important if you want to stand out in the crowd. This is a key factor in helping you achieve that goal. Do you want to be known as a copy? Well, in some cases, there are exceptions. For instance, if you're a singer, you may want to do a remake, which is completely acceptable as long as you get permission from the originator of the song. Just be mindful in everything you do and every approach you take, ensuring you're following the appropriate guidelines. The best and most effective approach in certain situations is simply being original. Being original will make you stand out and will separate you from the crowd. Keep in mind, depending on what you are aiming for, whether it be fame, fortune, or celebrity, you can achieve them if you put your mind to it, especially if you remain original.

Getting Uncomfortable

There are several things you can do to get uncomfortable. But first let's talk about why it's important to get uncomfortable. Being uncomfortable will help you grow as an individual. Yes, I know that this is not an easy task, and I expect some initial resistance. That's normal and to be expected. But think about how you learned to wear contact lenses or braces when you first had them. It took some getting used to. You had to start out learning how to get used to them until eventually it became a part of your daily routine. It became normal. It became comfortable. So let's look at how we can grow together and learn how to advance in our living. One way to get uncomfortable is to take a compliment. Yes, I know this sounds really simple. But just think about how a lot of people respond to compliments. Someone may say, "You have some pretty shoes," and your response would be "Oh, these old things?

I've had these for years." A better response could be "Thank you." Or what if someone says, "You have some pretty skin"? The response from someone struggling with self-esteem may be "You think so?" A more confident person may say, "I agree, and thank you so much." You see the difference in the responses? So another thing to consider when getting uncomfortable is gaining high self-esteem and self-confidence. You can do this by going to a class that works on that or using a coach. Just know that you are special and you matter. If you doubt yourself for any reason, think about your gift and how spectacular you are at using it, and use that as a self-esteem booster to your ego. Don't go overboard with that; just keep a humble spirit, and yes, watch the ego.

Another approach to getting uncomfortable could be taking Toastmasters or some public speaking class. You can learn to be presentable in front of an audience and how to cut out certain words or phrases that don't hold value to your message. Also, to get uncomfortable, think about waking up thirty minutes to an hour earlier to get things done quicker or to work on blocking out any unnecessary noise or potential distractions that could prevent your focus. This is something that a lot of successful people practice. You can be one.

Another way to getting uncomfortable is learning to accept constructive criticism. You don't want to be someone who doesn't like to be corrected when making mistakes. You want to learn from others, so allow people to tap into your area and give you the feedback you need to grow. You can also give constructive feedback. Don't just allow people to intervene in your life; step up and have a valuable opinion as well. This will work both ways, creating a win–win scenario for both parties. You can also attack conflict and win. When you have disagreement with someone, you can always agree to disagree. Don't be afraid to voice your opinion and listen to the other party's opinion as well. If you two can't come to terms on a mutual agreement, then just decide to accept the disagreement for what it is, an agreement to disagree!

You got it. Admit your mistakes, learn from them, and keep it moving. Don't linger on and on about how you were at fault. Just keep an open mind and know that everyone make mistakes. No one is perfect, so keep your head held high. Admit when you don't understand something or need something broken down for you. Keep at it and know that you are not the only one working on improving yourself. There are many people who want to grow. Hang around them.

Lastly, to get uncomfortable, face your fears head-on. Don't let them stop you from becoming the person God created you to be. Whatever your fear is, attack it head-on. Attack it first thing in the morning. Don't cave. You've got this. Come on, I know you can do it! Get uncomfortable!

Challenge Yourself

Challenge yourself to grow. Study your craft. Study others in your field, set timelines, and make big goals. Collaborate with others to push you and gain strengths. Don't give up. Find your creative process. Know what it is you want out of life and focus on that. Go for it. Review your work and rework your next work based on areas that need improvement. Be your own competition. Face your fears to help you overcome any obstacles. Don't procrastinate; focus on the ultimate goal. Don't just talk about what you want out of life; seize the moment. Seize the opportunities and shoot your shot. Go do what you are here to do and don't look back.

Competition

While in high school, I was very competitive, especially when it came to sports. I wanted to make sure I put in my best effort for the win. I was always told that second and third place didn't matter, so I wanted to make sure I played the best game in volleyball. I wanted to make sure I was the best dancer as a majorette, and for sure and I wanted to be the MVP in track. Well, when you're on your way to reaching your extreme destiny, you have to keep in mind that there will be competition, but the key here is knowing that you are your only competition. Don't compare, follow, or try to compete with anyone other than yourself. If you are an entertainer who put out videos for your music, review your last video and see what you can do differently to make the next one better. Do this for each video, focusing in on your particular body of work and no one else's. If you are an actor, review the footage from your last film and focus on how you can improve your delivery for your next take or next film. Don't make the mistake of competing with others. You are your only competition. Work on yourself on a regular basis to improve in areas where you feel you need to. Don't let the temptation of competing with others block you from receiving your blessing. Be competitive with yourself. You are your competition.

Modify Your Life

It's okay to imitate others you look up to as long as you don't take what they have done and make it your own. You learn from their mistakes and modify your life by amplifying what you believe needs to be enhanced. For example, I found a program similar to the one that I created to target young women with a dysfunctional relationship with their mothers. The program that I modified is similar, except it targets young women with a strained relationship with their fathers. It just made sense to use a similar format, and yes, I did get permission to do so before tackling the task, and so can you. If you are a singer and want to use lyrics from another artist's song, ask for permission. You will get a yes or no response. You can take this same approach with your life. If you know you have excelled and reached your potential with your life and feel you are fulfilled and loving life to the full, you can modify your life to reach another goal. So, if you would like to add more value to your life, focus on changes you can make to do so. Perhaps you could change your eating habits or learn a new skill. You could even join a new group that focuses on self-development or self-improvement. Whatever route you take, just think about ways that you can make changes to your life to better suit your needs and keep you fulfilled. You can modify your life by quitting smoking or stop using bad language when you're upset. Those are just some things you could do, but you have to do what's best for you and what will help you grow as an individual. You are worth so much more than your limitations, so use your better judgment when making major decisions on how to change things up for your life.

Increase Your Knowledge

The more information you consume and the more you know, the further you can go. Learn as much as you can about your area of expertise and interest. If you are just starting out as an actor and want to know more about the business, start out by taking some acting classes. Learn as much as you can about acting and whether or not you want to do theatre, TV, or film. Learn about them all and discover which one is best suited for your interest. As an actor, I've learned that you should learn it until you earn it. You want to learn as much as possible. People like the A-list star actors didn't get to where they are by just doing. They had to learn the craft. This applies to all areas of interest, not just acting. Get rid of lazy thinking and lack. Focus on the work. Even when you think you have learned it all, keep learning. You can do it. You don't necessarily have to enroll in a university to gain knowledge. You can simply study and research your area of interest through the internet or other credible sources. Little by little, every day, you can read new information. Invest in yourself. Accept full responsibility for where you are in life. A goal broken down with a date becomes a goal. A goal broken down into steps becomes a plan. A plan backed by action makes your dreams come true.

Apply Your Knowledge

Yes, I know you've heard that knowledge is power. In fact, when you take that same knowledge and apply it to your life, just imagine what you can do. The application of knowledge is power. The more information you apply, the further you go, the more valuable you become. Using the actor as an example again, use what you learned in your classes and workshops and apply that information to your auditions. Once you book a gig, apply those same lessons to your actual work on set or on the stage. You will be amazed at how much staying active in classes helps your presence on camera if you are considering film acting. Acting is not as simple as it may appear on television. There is a lot of work involved. You must put in the work if you want to gain the experience you desire. Wisdom will take you a long way. If you apply everything you know to your life, you have power. So begin to do so and watch your life change. For instance, if you have learned how to set goals better, to be more specific rather than a broad approach, you will have an advantage. Utilize the information from chapter 2 to actually write out your specific goal and execute the actual steps to make it a reality. Do the work.

Adding More Value

Increasing and applying knowledge adds value to your life. Consider this step a very significant one once you feel you have fulfilled your passion. You can add even more value by increasing your skill set. So, if you are good at typing, you can take a keyboarding class to increase the number of words you type per minute. If you are an athlete, you can increase your ability with a coach. There are numerous ways to add more value to your life; you want to grow and expand your horizons. You can start something new that allows you to grow in your personal life. You can set a goal to read a book every two weeks, or if you're bold, every week. You can learn something new, like how to improve your communication skills. All of these are just examples, but there are many other ways to add value to your life. Consider your individual self and what things you can do for your specific situation. Find your inspiration.

Change

Don't be afraid to change. It is a part of life. It can be difficult, but it is worth the effort. Work on self-development, change, and growth. You should be growing every three to five years. With growth comes change. Become a different person. Yes, you can do this. You can become a different person but only for the better. Who you spend time with is who you become. With this in mind, spend time with those who will help you grow. Spend time with those who know more than you. You are the solution to your problems. You are the answer. You are the cure. Who is to blame if you're not successful? You are. Don't blame anyone for your downfalls. Don't blame your parents, siblings, or teacher. It's on you, so hold yourself accountable. Build yourself up. Be the best at what you do. Master self-discipline. Once you master self-discipline, you become unstoppable. Reinvent yourself. Never be satisfied with yourself. You have unlimited potential. You can go as far in life as you desire and set your mind to. You are amazing! I know this is not an easy step, as it can be very challenging, especially when fear creeps in. That's why you have to allow your faith to guide you.

Are you growing? Have you advanced in your gift? Are you

leading the pack in your field? How significant have you become in your industry? What lessons have you learned through your journey? What are you worth? Have you gained anything during your journey of discovery? Have you had any breakthroughs?

Reinvent Yourself

A setback is a setup for a major comeback. Pace yourself and stay clear of conflict if possible. Aim to clear out physical clutter. Make your bed every morning and keep good hygiene while adding a new scent of fragrance to boost your confidence. Change your diet. You don't necessarily have to go on a diet, but you can minimize eating unhealthy foods like processed foods and sugar. Change up your routine. If you are a walker, maybe take a different route when working out and pick up the pace to a slight jog. Then later venture into a slight run, increasing your distance every so often as your body can handle it. Make yourself uncomfortable. You want to get out of your comfort zone and explore new experiences to have a new perspective. Sometimes this could mean a new environment, new friends, or even new ideas and thoughts. Express yourself. If you are a creative person, now is the time to show it through art, dance, or whatever you need to do to explore your creativity. Be assertive. When seeking to reinvent yourself, if you have questions, be assertive and face fear head-on. Work on tackling the most difficult tasks first. Be consistent. Don't change who you are to fit someone else's image of you. Cancel out the noise. You've got this!

Becoming More Attractive

When I say become more attractive, I'm not talking about your physical looks. I'm talking about your overall makeup of who you are and what you represent as a person. You want to make yourself more attractive when reinventing yourself. You can do this to improve the quality of your work. Your work is what you do that allows you to live out your purpose and get paid for it. Watch your habits. Make sure you are not careless about your habits. If there is a sign that says no loitering, don't throw a paper bag out. Place it in the nearest trash can. Be mindful of others' time. Don't show up late for your appointments. Watch what you say. There is a time and place for everything. Make sure you dress in appropriate attire for the occasion. Make sure your clothes are clean. Make sure you do not sabotage your opportunities by not thinking things through. Be professional. Work on your mindset to ensure you are keeping an upbeat, positive attitude toward life, even though trials and tribulations. Life is simply that, life. There will be things that happen that are out of your control. Put yourself first from time to time to ensure you are taking care of yourself and your needs. It's important that you treat yourself with kindness. Don't neglect the things you need to help nurture your gift. Empower others. Be determined. Study your role model. Remember your foundation and stay grounded. These things will help you become more attractive and unstoppable.

Becoming Unstoppable

Stop at nothing to reach your goals. You are more than a conqueror. You are a child of God, and you rock! Be so fierce in your work ethic. Practice until you have your niche to your degree of satisfaction. Respect yourself and don't let anyone discourage you. Conquer your fears. Conquer your fears by facing them and doing that which scares you. If that means taking the necessary baby steps to get to that point, do that. Own who you are. You are unstoppable, so don't shy away from that. Give attention only to the things that are deserving, and you will become unstoppable. Don't shy away from difficulties. Use them to overcome the challenges you face. Give your time and energy to those things that are of importance to you and don't waste time on things that don't serve you or your purpose. Become confident and secure in yourself, leaving all insecurities behind. Reject anything and anyone that makes you feel less than. Free yourself of any pain, hurt, or anything that can stand in your way of freedom and success. Use your imagination to be great. Allow it to become your reality and create your destiny. Celebrate you. Celebrate your successes and who you are and who you can become. Outwork your potential. Push yourself to become better. Practice and work on your craft every single day. Take action and execute what you have practiced. Be consistent in your efforts and always work on self-improvement. Spend time learning about those who are great and doing the same thing you desire to do. Observe your shortcomings and weaknesses and learn from them. Refocus and direct your attention to amplifying your strengths. Believe in yourself, because if you don't believe in yourself, no one else will. Maximize your efforts to the highest degree possible. I know you can do it, if you just put your mind to it and focus. I believe in you.

Protect Your Dream

As an actor, it is important to be in the moment when performing. Just be. Use this same approach to any field you're interested in and learn to just be with yourself. Love yourself. Protect your energy. Make sure you are giving your all and nothing less, without losing yourself or what you stand for. Stay away from negativity, negative people, and negative environments. You want to center yourself around like-minded people who have your best interests at heart. Choose your tribe wisely and be mindful of who you share your dreams with. Write your dreams down and look at it first thing in the morning and last thing at night before you go to bed.

Secrets to Staying Relevant

Take breaks. Take breaks to give people a breather and allow them to miss you. Reinventing yourself helps you stay relevant, but avoid overdoing it. But is there really ever too much of anything? The answer to that question is up to you. But learning something new can help you in this area also. You can consider a makeover. You can upgrade yourself. Exercise more for a healthier lifestyle. Come out of your shell. If you are an entertainer, read up on other entertainers' success and apply the lessons learned to your life. Gain experience. Go to networking events. Stay current on new technologies that apply to your craft. Get an accountability partner. Learn and apply the latest technologies and trends. Stay on top of things that are relevant to your specific area of gifting or purpose. Restructure strategies that are no longer popular or that don't work or serve a purpose for you. Keep your network informed, involved, and motivated. Overcommunicate your needs to your team. Stay social but don't allow roadblocks to interfere with your progress. Asking someone new for help in your area of expertise can help advance your career. After you have utilized your resources and experience a drought, you can replenish by seeking counsel from someone who has more experience and expertise to shed some new light on your situation. Use teasers. Let people see only a certain amount of you until the big reveal. Be productive.

Productivity

After achieving some level of success while on your journey, it's time to measure your productivity. The first thing you want to do is determine who your target market is. Who do you want to reach while using your gift or purpose? Next, implement your research into actionable items, making sure you follow your specific goals while being consistent in your efforts. You can do this by creating a timeline to meet your goals and check items off your list as you complete them. You want to make sure you are being as productive as possible with your time because your time is valuable, and you don't want to waste any of it. Keep in mind that your goal is to operate in your purpose and to serve others just as God wants. Avoid spending time doing meaningless things. Avoid going to events that serve no purpose. Avoid hanging with or spending time with people who don't have your best interests at heart. You want to make sure that everything you do is in alignment with your goals and aspirations. Keep a journal of your events and activities and reread your progress every six months. Look for areas that need improvements and adjust accordingly.

Asking for Help

When my daughter was younger, she used to always try to do things by herself. Whenever anyone would offer to help her, she would continue to try to solve the problem by herself. My dad noticed this, and we immediately began to direct her to ask for help. You want to make sure you are not centering your only source to be you. Your source is God. Yes, you can seek help from family, friends, colleagues, and many others, but don't forget that God is your complete resource. If you pray to him for everything you need and seek his kingdom, you will have everything you need, including the necessary help. Don't be too proud to ask for help or guidance. You know the Bible says pride comes before destruction, so keep that in the back of your mind when you feel that pride setting in. You will be glad you reached out in the end.

Being Patient

Patience is one of the most necessary character traits to have and is one of the most valuable. It will take you a long way in life, especially if you are an actor or salesperson. Being patient can help you overcome any situation or obstacle. Patient people have a higher rate of return on desired results. They are more likely to explore more opportunities and take different routes to success. For instance, if you are patient as an actor and allow yourself to develop and grow, you will reap the benefits of sacrificing other things that you may have wanted to do. This is just a part of the process. Don't get discouraged and don't give up. Give yourself room to allow for mistakes. Learn from them and keep it moving. Some things you may sacrifice are listed below in the next section. Keep reading, my friend. You've got this.

Sacrifice

Everyone has the potential to do something great, but in order to be great, you have to make sacrifices. You have to make sacrifices for your family, loved ones, friends, colleagues, and even yourself. I remember a time I was supposed to meet my best friend. We had it all planned out. I would drive, and we would have dinner and just enjoy each other's company. We had made plans for our children, and everything was planned out at least a few weeks in advance, until I had to cancel due to a film I got the opportunity to work on. I was all worked up, saying, "Aw, man, my friend is gonna be disappointed." She was very understanding, and that is what made all the difference, and I knew I could make it up to her later. When you are committed to your craft, it takes making sacrifices to get to the level you are aiming for. Make sure you have understanding people in your corner who can work with you.

There will come a time when you have to make sacrifices

while pursuing your purpose. You may have to sacrifice time, energy, and sleep. Whatever you do, don't sacrifice your health. Without health, you can't continue on. Know that when you live within your purpose and follow God's lead, there are some sacrifices that take place. It may mean you will not be able to hang out with friends like you used to. You may have to use that time to focus on your craft. It could mean that you can't go to parties or on vacation as much as you want to or used to. You may consider using that energy and effort on your purpose. You do need to get sleep, but I understand sometimes that you may get in your zone and lose some. Just make sure to make up for it when you can so you can be as productive as possible. You may have to sacrifice finances as well to apply them to more important things. For instance, maybe you used to eat out a lot. Now, you may consider cooking at home and reserve that income for acting classes or new headshots. Just keep in mind that at some point in your career, you will need to make a sacrifice to be successful. Don't fret; it will pay off in the end if you love what you do.

Love What You Do

If you don't naturally love what you do, you may want to reconsider if you're actually passionate about your craft. But I would think at this point that you have found your passion and you do love it. It should be something that ignites an unexplainable feeling inside of you and drives you to greatness. It should light your fire. Have faith in yourself and your efforts and know that you are special, and therefore, the energy you put out in the universe is special. So love yourself and love your work. If you don't believe in and love your work, no one else will. Don't make excuses and don't procrastinate. Just get the job done and live with no regrets. Find your confidence. If you are doing what you love, this step should be easy. If you are confident in your purpose and doing what you love, you have an advantage. Be fully committed in your craft. Don't half step. Put in significant effort and know that it will pay off in the end. Embrace who you are and know that you are good enough. Be your own support and support team. Cheer for yourself and know that you are valuable.

Back to the Basics

Remember your foundation—attitude, mind-set, and determination—when you need to stay grounded. Stay the course and don't get off track if at all possible. If you need your mom, dad, role model, mentor, or whoever keeps you grounded like an accountability partner, make sure they are in the know of what you are trying to do with your purpose. For me, that person is God. I do have coaches and mentors who have helped me, and I am eternally grateful for each and every one of them. My dad and grandmother were my biggest supporters while they were still living, and I know they still watch over me from above.

The next thing you want to do when considering change while pursing your extreme destiny is to take baby steps to get the results you want. Stick to the fundamentals. Begin with your prayer, asking God to show you where you can take your career to next. Then, if you need to go on a fast, let that be your next step. Challenge yourself. Don't lose yourself, but rather focus on how to grow. Pay attention to your intentions and know what the purpose of your actions are. If you change your perspective and regroup, you can have a clearer view of what you want. Learn to appreciate others and the love and support they give you. There will be times when people will help you if you allow them. Treat others the way you want to be treated and remember where you came from. Remember the reason you wanted to take the journey of your craft in the first place. Know your purpose. Remember the foundational work you put in and regroup as necessary. Put others first and be grateful for everything that you have, even the little things.

Baby Steps

When considering change, start with a small effort with the knowledge you have gained and take baby steps to apply it to your life. Just a few. One step at a time. Take it slowly, one day at a time, praying to God to lead you every step of the way. Have patience and give yourself time to push through. Continue to break down goals into pieces. Baby steps. You have to approach change as if you're eating an elephant, eating one bite at a time. Think back to chapter 1 and remember how you should approach self-discovery, by uncovering your unique you by discovering your gifts, knowing your talents, being of service, being yourself, living with no expectations, having limitless faith, overcoming hardship, and allowing yourself to be in your element. You have to take each of these areas one step at a time, day by day. Don't try to attack them all at once; you will get overwhelmed. Just have patience and work your way through each one, step by step. You will be glad you did in the end. So trust the process. Focus on each day. One move at a time. You can easily get distracted and try to look at the big picture when your focus should be taking each item one day at a time. Come on! You can do this!

Share Your Knowledge, Gifts, Talents, and Purpose with Others

Don't be selfish. Let others in on how you made it to where you are. The benefits are so rewarding. Help others. Share your lessons learned with others. Do you know how important you are? You are valuable to the world. You are an example of what it's like to have meaning and happiness. You are a blessing to God. Make him proud by living out his vision for your life. Don't give up. Don't give in. Keep faith and hope that you are his child and he loves you. Don't leave this earth not living your full potential. Live your best life and be a blessing to others. You deserve it. Just imagine what the world would be like without you. There would be a void. You mean so much to others. Don't ever lose sight of that and be all that God created you to be, even when you don't feel like it. Push through. You've got this. Yes, it's okay to take breaks, but don't quit.

So what is life like living your extreme destiny? Less crime. Just think. People would be doing what they love, living a fulfilled life and loving themselves for it. They wouldn't have time to think about robbing someone or killing. They would be consumed with what they love. So how about it. Let's change the world. Let's do something to help people learn their purpose. At this point in your journey, if you are depressed, then you are not utilizing your gift. Do not follow the crowd. Find your gift. If you can find your purpose, you can discover your gift.

Reread this material until you grasp why you were put on this earth. Do not give up! I repeat—do not give up. You are important. You are valuable, and you matter. If you have found your purpose and are living your extreme destiny, kudos to you! Keep it up. If you have not, what are you waiting for? Go get yours! So what problem did you solve with your gift?

Potential

Who am I? Why am I here? What's my purpose for living? Where am I from? Where am I going? Why do I stand out? These are questions that help determine your potential in life. Potential is having or showing the capacity to become something in the future. You may live in your purpose and still can develop into something greater than what you have ever imagined. You should aspire to be greater than your greatest accomplishment. You have the power of the pen, so utilize it to map out your blueprint for the life you desire and deserve. You, without purpose, is like you without life or breath. Your potential is tied into your purpose to a higher degree. It is what you can become, not what you are. So, yes, you could be a speaker, but your potential may be that you are a motivational speaker in several countries. Aim high and reach for the stars in everything you do, giving God the credit and maximizing your potential to be the greatest of the great. You have the potential to do what you believe in. If you can think it, you can do it. Whatever it is. If you believe you can do it, then you can and you will.

You Have to Want It

At this point, you should really want to excel at your craft. If you find that what you have discovered is not what you really want, you should reread the previous chapters. You have to have something so strong within you that an extreme desire overpowers you, to the degree that you want it so badly you become unstoppable in your efforts to obtain it. Don't give up on your dreams. Take responsibility for your God-given gift. You have to have something deep within you that makes you want it so badly that your love for it is unexplainable. Be driven. Seize the opportunities as they come and don't take anything for granted. Have a strong why so that you can sustain your faith and belief in your passion. Enjoy your craft and make sure you are putting substantial effort in making sure you are being authentic.

Working on Your Craft

Work on your craft when no one is watching. Work on your craft even when you don't feel like it. Invest in your craft. Invest in yourself and your efforts to achieve satisfaction with your craft. Fail and fail big. Don't be afraid to face failure head-on, leading you into what God has for you. Study. Study the best. Put your efforts into gaining so much experience that you surprise yourself with your results. You are magnificent and bring so much to the table. Work like you have so much in store that you can't abuse your time. Time is valuable, and you want to make sure you are using it to its full and not wasting any of it if you can help it. Make no excuse and put your efforts strategically in a place that serves your purpose. Love the process. It's the process that will allow you to learn and grow, but you must appreciate it just as much as you appreciate yourself. Have a great work ethic and use that energy to be your best at your craft. Your purpose is so much more than just being for you. It is for others. People need to see you succeeding and winning so that they have hope that they too can take a path to living their extreme destiny. Working on your craft will give others the hope they need to succeed as well.

Giving Credit

Say thank you, and say it often. Give credit where credit is due. You did not do this alone. If you think you have done this on your own, you are mistaken. First and foremost, there would be no you without God. Also, consider that you wouldn't exist if your parents didn't give birth to you. Everyone has some help along the way, whether they want to believe it and accept it or not. Even though I had some trials in my younger years, I still had a support system that helped me through life. Whether it was my guidance counselor or advice from a childhood friend, pastor, mentor, or coach, someone extended a hand to help, and I'm sure you can think of at least one person who has done the same for you. Some ways of giving credit are as follows:

- Send a thank-you card in the mail or by email.
- Give an arrangement of flowers.
- Give a shout out on a chosen platform like social media.
- Simply say, "Thank you."

Sending a thank-you card makes for a personal touch. Not too many people are doing this anymore, so it means that much more. You can also send an electronic thank you by email, and it will have a nice effect as well. Giving a nice flower arrangement to a mentor or coach or someone who has had a major impact in your life makes them feel appreciated. If you want to be bold like me and make a thank-you post or shout out on social media, it will have a major effect because your followers witness that as well. Simply saying thank you is a much appreciated approach as well. All of these ways of giving credit are remarkable and say a lot about who you are, so don't shortchange anyone and do this in every area of your life for everyone who has contributed to your success. Keeping in mind that initially you may not have any support because people are looking to see you take off and become successful. Don't let this stop you. Just because people don't initially believe in you doesn't mean they will not do it later. Keep doing what you're doing and don't let up. Root for others to win while fulfilling your assignment.

Fulfill Your Assignment

Don't be someone who lets your gifts and talents go unused or unnoticed. You deserve the opportunity to share with others and be valued for it through God's will. I pray you lead a legacy in fulfilling your assignment. You don't want to leave this world not fulfilling your purpose. There are so many people who never tap into their purpose and live a miserable life of lack, resentment, and regret in old age. Don't let this be you. You deserve so much more, and it's not about you. It's about sharing what you were blessed with with the rest of the world so that they too can be blessed. You can encourage and motivate so many others by just using your gift. It doesn't matter how old or young you are; you can explore and live out your destiny if you focus on doing just that. Fulfill your assignment so that you can be the difference in someone else's life while changing and impacting the world.

Excel

Don't compare yourself to others. Focus on your passion and work it. Continuously work on your craft and love what you do. Be genuine about your intentions. Practice until you feel confident in your efforts for pursing your passion. If you study and practice your craft on a daily basis, you will gain confidence and began to excel. The key to exceling in your craft is to gradually work on your craft on a daily basis until you reach the desired result or goal.

Killer Instinct

You have to train your mind to be fearless. Expect excellence of yourself. Don't allow anything other than greatness to enter your space. Don't allow procrastination or laziness to be an issue for you. Learn from the best. Bring the fire that lives within you. Be curious and figure out new approaches to getting things done. You want success? Take it. It's yours—if you truly want it. Be fierce yet sincere and honest. Don't hurt anyone in the process. Break records. Score points. Love your passion and love it hard. Listen to your gut and instincts when making decisions. You're the master of your fate.

Standing Out

Keep track of where you spend your time and effort. Be different. Don't chase money and don't chase people. Chase your dreams with full capacity, knowing your worth it. Be mindful in knowing what your dream is and knowing that your dream is worthy of you. Have a solid morning routine that you follow every day regardless of what's going on. Have a routine that works for you and commit to it. Ask yourself, "Why?" Why do you do what you do? Why is this important to you? Redefine what you have already discovered in the previous chapters of this book and let the reason for your why be what drives you. Get discipline in your area of expertise and manage your time well. Say no when necessary and say yes when necessary. Don't allow others' opinions of you to stop you from achieving success. Do things that scare you on a regular basis and give in to the things that will help you grow and be unique and rare. Do something different that adds value to your life and continue to work at your passion for the fulfillment of reaching your extreme destiny.

Doing Something Different

Doing something different will allow you to stand out. You have to reprogram your thinking when trying to learn something new. Allow others to help you in this transition. Learn to get to know yourself and know what your strengths and weaknesses are. Develop a plan of attack to address the things that you want to work on. Take control of your life, leading it with full force and allowing your inner strength to rise. Give yourself space to focus on a path that is different but that can strengthen the growth of your purpose or passion. Don't get comfortable with the norm. Don't get complacent to where you begin to follow the crowd and forget your reasoning behind your actions. Do the hard work and put the time in, and that will separate you from the pack.

Being the Best

Go hard. Get serious. Stop with the games. Get real. Have an extreme work ethic and do your absolute best. Have a mind-set that will push you to be the best. Always work on evolving into a better version of yourself. You can do great things if you put your mind to it. You are great. Don't hesitate to put your best foot forward. Compliment yourself on your efforts and treat yourself for your accomplishments. Do. The. Work. Go all out. Perfect your craft. Put in all your effort to be the best. Make your sacrifices and don't let up on reaching the level of desired success. You hold the cards to reaching your extreme destiny. Play them, and play them well. Express yourself and share with the world. Do the right thing. Focus on the things that bring you closer to your vision. Find courage within yourself and be courageous. Love yourself and love others. Have thick skin. Find your inspiration. Be a blessing to others. Turn your hardships, trials, and struggles into triumphs. Always do your best. Live with no regrets. Have a secret talent and have fun with it. Love to work. Become your best self. Redefine yourself for the better at every opportunity you can. Make people notice you. Abandon the things that make you comfortable. You are valued, and people will love you for it. You've earned it! Don't stop.

Obeying God

This is a topic that is probably the most challenging one—obeying God. God is our source for everything. He gave us life through our parents and created us through his image. Let's be clear, he is King of all kings and Lord of all lords. He should be named your number one. Therefore, we should do our best to obey his Word. I know that we are only human and are sinners by nature, but let's do our best to keep him happy and satisfied. We can do this by reading his Word and gaining the knowledge needed to ensure we follow through with his commands. Keep in mind that he is also a forgiving God, so if you just so happen to sin, know that repentance is an option. Be all that he created you to be. Take everything that he has put in your heart and honor him by being faithful and true to yourself. Know that you are special and unique and deserve the best, as he is willing to help you get just that when you obey him.

Drive

What drives you? What pushes you to your max? What makes you think outside the box? What generates something so powerful in you that you can't resist? Let's talk. Drive is a desire that pushes or encourages you. Think about what pushes you to want to excel in everything you do. Whatever that looks like, whatever that is, use that as a driving force for reaching your extreme destiny. It could be certain music that drives you. Or maybe it's a certain motivational speech or speaker that influences you. Keep that message on replay when you are ready to get in your element, for it will be the driving force that helps you reach your climax while on your journey to your extreme destiny. Let whatever drives you and your love for God guide you to your destination of living your best life.

Image

What image are you trying to relay? What is image? Image is the representation of you. How do you want to present yourself to the public? What are you striving to portray? Would you like to be an A-list actor? Would you like to be a professional athlete? Would you like to be a comedian? Whatever you intend to represent or strive for represents who you are and is your image. Maintaining consistency in your efforts for your gift will help you maintain your image. If you are continually showing who you really are on a constant basis, you make a habit out of that, and people will notice. My college theatre director once told me that if you don't want to be known for going out in the club, then stay out of the club. Unless someone is blatantly lying on you, he has a point. If you don't want to be known as a politician, then stay out of politics. Choose your battles wisely. Step away from fights and things that will damage your image. Focus on being someone of integrity who follows through, especially when you say you're going to do something. If you feel you can't commit, then communicate that. Remember who you are. When on social media, think before posting, especially if what you want to post could potentially be offensive. A rule of thumb you could use is maybe have a list of items to cross off before making a post. Your list could consist of items like these:

1. Does this reflect who I want to portray?
2. Does this represent my goals?
3. How will this impact my overall image?

You could add as many items as you would like. Just keep in mind that it is personal to your needs and the specific image that you want to maintain. You can also evolve, so don't ever feel like you're stuck being one way. Be courageous and go all out but maintain who you really are and stay true to yourself. Use your better judgment to make sure that you are being true to yourself and what you represent. Don't be a people pleaser; only please you and God, and you will go far. There will be others trying to tell you what you should be like and who you should be. Don't let them. Allow what you feel best represents who you are to take precedence, having the final say in what image you want to portray. You can do it.

Never Give Up

Focus. Create the life you want and train yourself to implement your daily oriented goals with discipline. Control your thoughts, your mind-set, and the level in which you believe in yourself. Let nothing and no one stop you from achieving what you set out to achieve. Allow yourself to grow fearlessly because you are worth it. You are worth so much more than where you are at in your life today, and the more drive and hunger you have for your craft, the better off you will be. Whatever you do, don't give up because you never know what you are capable of and who you can become.

Build Yourself Up

How do you build yourself up? Well, first and foremost, you have to look at things in a certain sequence. For instance, if you want to become an actor, then you can map out your end goal as to how far you want to take your acting career. Then plan the previous steps that you need to take to get to that point. There are so many pieces that play a role in reaching your final destination, and you have to know what those things are and follow the steps to get there. You can practice and study to build yourself up to make sure you are where you need to be in your passion. Set boundaries and learn from your mistakes so that you don't repeat them. Work on your inner beauty to become more than what others see on the outside. Shine from within, using the faith that you have of who you are and who you are becoming and what you are meant to be. You are meant to be great and do great things. Don't concern yourself with what others think you should be; aspire to be what you believe in your heart you are supposed to be. Demand respect and eliminate the need to please. Don't worry about what people feel about you. Focus on your inner strength and growth and know that you are worth it. Know that there is a power greater than yourself, and if you can connect to that power, you will excel. Anything is possible, if you just believe. Your legacy is every life you've touched, so go ahead and inspire someone else while you build yourself up.

Outwork Your Potential

Ask why something didn't work out. When one way no longer works, figure out another way. You are your potential and what's inside you, and what you believe about yourself will take you a long way. Your potential is more than what you are capable of. It is the thing you can do that you have yet to discover. It is the thing you have embedded deep within you that is to be uncovered. When you discover your potential, you have to go further and outwork it by being an overachiever. Being an overachiever takes commitment, faith, and belief. You can do it, if you put your mind to it.

Trusting Yourself

Now that you have gained all this information and these strategies for living your best life, you have to trust yourself. As a former athlete, I learned to use my struggles as a weapon to overcome and maximize my potential to the fullest. Sleepless nights, long, strenuous workouts, and many other things that took place during my early years led me to have the drive I have now to pursue my goals to the fullest. I trust myself to do my best with every effort I put into my goals, and so can you.

Live Your Best Life

Are you crazy enough to think you can live your best life?
Now for some housekeeping rules. Whatever you do, don't

take life for granted. Make sure you have good manners. Speak to everyone you come in contact with, including the janitor and maid. Don't think you are better or less than the next person. Look people in the eye when speaking with them and shaking their hands. Be grateful, even for the little things. Pray for wisdom. Center yourself around those who believe in you. All it takes is one. There is no hiding. You are who you are at day and at night. Don't try to be a different person to different people. Don't try to act a certain way for a certain expectation. Live with no expectations. Don't be afraid to shine and show who you really are. Celebrate your accomplishments and then keep it moving and create more. Stay humble, stay grounded, and stay hungry. Take time to rest. Don't get burnt out. Don't accept your current situation as your final destination. Only accept things that you believe in and nothing less. That opportunity fell through? So what. It was for your protection. Keep moving. Create and leave your legacy. Never accept no as an answer. You want to live your extreme destiny by being healthy, living a healthy lifestyle, being quick to forgive, knowing why you were created, and living in your gift and purpose. This will make you powerful!

Just Keep Going

If you haven't learned anything from this book, just know this. You're going to have good moments, bad moments, and in-between moments. Whichever one you have, keep going. You can learn from someone else with a passion and draw from that to empower yourself. I'm not talking about imitating someone; I'm talking about gaining motivation from others who are passionate about what they do. This will help make you better at living your passion. I cannot encourage this enough, but hire a coach. A coach can help you take your career to the next level. They can fast-track your goals by pushing you beyond your current state.

Use a mentor. You can learn a lot from a mentor. Just know that they can be a source of encouragement in a time of need.

Outwork Others—The Turning Point

When you have reached a certain point in life and have accomplished your goals, you have reached a turning point. That means it's now time to find new challenges. It's time to face those obstacles and stumbling blocks that got in your way. It's time to move forward on a different level. You can rise above any situation by believing in the fact that you can. As simple as it sounds, it does take commitment, and I know you can do it. If you are an athlete and you are running a race where there are first, second, and third places, think about what sets you aside from the others. What makes you great? When you can, tap into that thing that will give you the push you need to work hard, practice, and study your strengths and your competition at this point. When you study your competition, you learn their strengths, strategies, and weaknesses and can use that as a guide to add value to your approach of attack. This attack is a technique you can use to have the upper hand. When trying to get first place in a track meet, focus on the time of your competition compared to your fastest time and practice until you beat the fastest time. This will give you the strength to win and outwork others. Take responsibility for your actions. Give more than the next guy. "But wait," you say. "You said I am my only competition." Yes, that is true, but in the case of the athlete seeking first, second, or third place, you have to consider the other runners' time to beat.

Hard Times

Jonathan woke up to a screaming baby and immediately jumped out of bed and stumbled on a red and yellow Lego. He looked over to his right and remembered that his wife had a doctor's appointment that he forgot about. He also remembered that he forgot to reschedule a meeting for a later time so he could watch the children until his wife returned. His day was off to a rough start.

What would you do in the situation that Jonathan found himself in? Would you scream and get frustrated or calmly handle things the best way you know how?

Expect hard times. Prepare for them and learn to deal with them. Hard times might be a bad day with a headache. It could mean you woke up late or forgot to meditate, so that threw your day off. When things like this happen, you have to be conscious of how you respond. If you have a negative response to hard times or struggles, it will weigh you down and sometimes cause depression or even illness. But if you have a positive attitude, it can change the direction of your day for the better. Just keep your mind-set and thought process in perspective when these types of things happen. You are in control of your destiny, not the issue at hand.

Accepting Life

Accept life for what it is. Life. Life is full of processes, challenges, obstacles, transitions, changes, things, love, patience, inconsistencies, and so on. You name it, it all exists. It is what it is. It is life. We all have to live it. So when things get tough, know that someone else is going through something worse. Maybe someone is going through something similar and can relate to you. Or maybe you are the first to experience it. Jump in. Don't be afraid to tackle life and take it for what it is, a part of life. Everyone faces it, whether we want to or not.

Win

Accept that you are a winner, with strength and determination. Don't let failure stop you from accomplishing your goals in life. Failure is a part of the process. The sooner you accept this, the better off you will be. Everyone has their season. Just because things may not be working out right now for you doesn't mean that they won't work out in the near future. That could be tomorrow, next week, next month, next year, or two years from now. Either way, eventually you will have a winning season, and you, my dear, will shine. So don't be afraid to win. Develop an insane work ethic to the degree that it becomes an everyday lifestyle. It becomes a habit and is a part of who you are. Work on your craft daily, implementing small advances every day, challenging yourself as much as possible until you have to grab an outsider to push you to do more when necessary. If you are working out your body and need guidance to reach a desired result, start out slowly and increase your potential by using a personal trainer or health coach. You will be surprised at the results you can get when you utilize other resources to maximize what's already in you.

The Power of Love

Spread love in every way possible. Love your neighbor, love your family, love your friends, love your enemies, and love yourself. Just love, and know that others love you as well, even if they don't say it. And when all else fails, know that God loves you. When you show love to others by sharing your gifts and talents, you become a light to those who may not have direction in their lives. Don't be afraid of the power of love. When you love others just as you love yourself, you honor God, and he is pleased.

Helping Others

You can help others by sharing your story and giving pointers, tips, and advice on how you became who you are. You can become someone's mentor. You can talk about what challenges you overcame and what steps you took to overcome them. You can express your hardships and how they impacted you and what you did to get to where you are today. Discuss your everyday obstacles, like how you deal with a nagging spouse, or how you instruct your children in difficult times. Inspire others and pray for others.

Give Back

Now that you are powerful, let's declare a selfless act of love by giving to those who are less fortunate. Most importantly, think about a cause you would like to support and give to. Maybe you want to give to a charity or your local church or a foundation for a certain cause. Make a difference in someone's life.

There are different ways to give back. You can volunteer your time or maybe even your gift. Either way, you will be doing a good deed, and others will appreciate you more for this act of kindness. The feeling of giving back is like no other. One of my goals in life is to leave a legacy that allows others to grow into what God has designed them to be. I embraced my willpower, determination, and the traits in this book, and for that, I did get the perfect attendance after constantly hassling the board of education about that one day I showed up to McKissack Middle sick. I hope you have learned enough to carry you into what God has created you to be. I hope you have been inspired and encouraged to do just that. Live your extreme destiny!

So that's my journey and my tips on how to live your extreme destiny. I hope you have learned something that you can apply to your journey in life. If not, feel free to reach out; let's have a conversation. If so, great! I want you to take what you have learned here and apply it to your everyday life. After completing these steps, if you are still not where you want to be in life, don't blame others. Don't make excuses. It's not anybody's fault. You have to look in the mirror and look back on the choices you made throughout your journey. If you already knew everything in this book but know someone who could use the material, pass it along to a friend or family member. Most importantly, just be happy. So are you ready to live your extreme destiny? To those who are ready to take the leap into a new journey, sit back, buckle up, and get ready because you're up! It's your season to live your extreme destiny! Godspeed!

DECLARATION OF LOVE

I love myself today. I am in love with who I am and what I am about. I am great! I am enough! I stand for greatness! I am God's child, and you better know that God loves me just as I am!

DON'T QUIT
By John Whittier

When things go wrong as they sometimes will,
When the road you're trudging seems all uphill,
When the funds are low and the debts are high,
And you want to smile, but you have to sigh,
When care is pressing you down a bit,
Rest, if you must, but don't you quit.
Life is strange with its' twists and turns,
As every one of us sometimes learns,
And many a failure turns about,
When he might have won had he stuck it out;
Don't give up though the pace seems slow—
You may succeed with another blow.
Success is failure turned inside out—
The silver tint of the clouds of doubt,
And you never can tell how close you are,
It may be near when it seems so far,
So stick to the fight when you're hardest hit—
It's when things seem worst that you must not quit.

INSPIRATIONAL QUOTES

Change will not come if we wait for
some other person or some other time.
We are the ones we've been waiting for.
We are the change that we seek.
—Barack Obama

Success isn't about how much money
you make. It's about the difference
you make in people's lives.
—Michelle Obama

I remember my first agent telling me—
because they found me as an actor, but I
was probably more interested in writing
and maybe directing—they were like,
"Well you can't do both things." And
I was like, "I'm gonna show you."
—Chadwick Boseman

I never lose, I either win or learn.
—Nelson Mandela

Your self-worth is determined by
you. You don't have to depend on
someone telling you who you are.
—Beyoncé

Why live an ordinary life, when you
can live an extraordinary one.
—Tony Robbins

Even though you're fed up, you
gotta keep your head up.
—Tupac Shakur

You have to do the thing that terrifies you.
—Octavia Spencer

You get what you give. What you put into
things is what you get out of them.
—Jennifer Lopez

When your foundation is faith,
you become undefeated.
—Toni C. Hughes

I don't want no one telling me
how to live my life.
—Malayia I. Morrow

Anything you can imagine you can create.
—Oprah Winfrey

Great things come from hard work
and perseverance. No excuses.
—Kobe Bryant

Acting is my calling, not my career.
—Angela Bassett

I am different. I am an original. And like
everyone else, I am here to take up space
from the universe. I do so with pride.
—Shonda Rhimes

You pray for rain, you gotta deal with
the mud too. That's a part of it.
—Denzel Washington

Make your life a masterpiece; imagine no
limitations on what you can be, have or do.
—Brian Tracy

If opportunity doesn't knock, build a door.
—Milton Berle

A woman is like a teabag—only in hot
water do you realize how strong she is.
—Nancy Reagan

PRAYER FOR PEACE

I pray for peace in your life as you pursue your God-driven purpose and live out your extreme destiny. I pray you find what you're looking for way deep down in the depths of your soul, with peace and patience. May God direct your path. In Jesus's name. Amen.

AFFIRMATIONS

I am enough.
I am more than enough.
I am valuable.
I am loved.
I am driven.
I am valued.
I am blessed.
I am unique.
I am gifted.
I am God's child.

A PRAYER FOR SOMEONE IN
SEARCH OF THEIR PURPOSE

Heavenly father, I come to you for clarity,
Clarity for the plan you have for my life.
I am seeking guidance on how to walk the
path you have destined for me.
I surrender my all to you.
I put my trust in you.
Please show me the way to living my extreme destiny
in the purpose you have for me, as you see fit.
In Jesus's name.
Amen.

THE GREATEST IN THE LAND

As I seek your kingdom, I know that you
are the greatest in all the land,
For you are the King of kings
The Lord of lords,
And I put my faith and trust in you.

A PROMISE

I promise to use my gift before I die.
I promise to use my gift to the fullest.
I promise to be consistent in using my gift.
I promise to follow through.
I promise to never give up.
I promise.

Live the life you deserve ...

Are you wondering what you were placed on this earth to do? Do you sit and wish you were living your best life to the fullest? Do you ever think about what it would be like to know exactly why God placed you on this earth? Are you feeling lack and incomplete in your current job? Would you like to know how to reach your extreme destiny?

This essential guide will help you learn how to find your true purpose and passion in life. You'll learn different strategies to find the true meaning of why you were placed on this earth. Rather than staying stuck in a career that brings resentment and void, you will learn to live your passion and live your life to the fullest.

Toni C. Hughes is a native of Nashville, Tennessee, currently residing in Summerville, South Carolina. She is an actor, author, and entrepreneur who has worked as a computer scientist for the Department of Defense. She is a living example of what it's like to live in your purpose and live a life led by passion and love for her craft. Her motto is "inspire, impact, and change lives." Her desire in life is to help others achieve and live a life of authenticity while pursuing their passion. She also holds a B.S. in computer science from Tennessee State University and an M.S. in science management with an emphasis in project management from Strayer University. She has two children, Malik and Malayia. She is driven by her faith in God and love for her craft of being a creative.

—Toni C Hughes, Introduction

"Toni packs a lot of wisdom in her book, *Living Your Extreme Destiny*, especially on the topics of passion and purpose. The energy of passion, combined with the direction of purpose, will allow you to tap into your extreme destiny and live your fullest life."

—Karen Putz, author of *Unwrapping Your Passion, Creating the Life You Truly Want*

"*Living Your Extreme Destiny* is an inspiring and motivational guide. Toni does an amazing job sharing her own personal journey of discovering her true gifting and provides readers with a detailed road map on how to do the same."

—Ursula Burroughs, MBA, PT, CWC, author of *Little Is Much in the Father's Hands*

Please feel free to leave a review or comment at lyedofficial@outlook.com or livingyourextremedestiny@outlook.com
For more information, go to www.tonichughes.com
Follow Toni on Twitter: @hughestonic
Follow Toni on Instagram: @tonichughes
Like Toni on Facebook: Facebook.com/hughestonic
Visit Toni's imdb page: www.imdb.me/tonichughes
Visit Toni's blog: http://tonichughes.tumblr.com
Cover photo credit: Michelle Bryant Griffin

Printed in the United States
By Bookmasters